ce

# bright ideas in papercrafts

susan niner janes

David & Charles

# bright ideas in papercrafts

**A DAVID & CHARLES BOOK**

First published in the UK in 2003
First published in the USA in 2003 by North Light Books,
Cincinnati, Ohio

ISBN 0 7153 1739 3

Printed in China by Leefung-Asco
for David & Charles
Brunel House    Newton Abbot    Devon

Visit our website at www.davidandcharles.co.uk

David & Charles books are available from all good bookshops;
alternatively you can contact our Orderline on (0)1626 334555 or
write to us at FREEPOST EX2 110, David & Charles Direct, Newton
Abbot, TQ12 4ZZ (no stamp required UK mainland).

Editor: David Oeters
Designer: Joanna Detz
Layout Artist: John Langan
Production Coordinator: Michelle Ruberg
Photographers: Christine Polomsky, Tim Grondin and Al Parrish

## METRIC CONVERSION CHART

| TO CONVERT | TO | MULTIPLY BY |
|---|---|---|
| Inches | Centimeters | 2.54 |
| Centimeters | Inches | 0.4 |
| Feet | Centimeters | 30.5 |
| Centimeters | Feet | 0.03 |
| Yards | Meters | 0.9 |
| Meters | Yards | 1.1 |
| Sq. Inches | Sq. Centimeters | 6.45 |
| Sq. Centimeters | Sq. Inches | 0.16 |
| Sq. Feet | Sq. Meters | 0.09 |
| Sq. Meters | Sq. Feet | 10.8 |
| Sq. Yards | Sq. Meters | 0.8 |
| Sq. Meters | Sq. Yards | 1.2 |
| Pounds | Kilograms | 0.45 |
| Kilograms | Pounds | 2.2 |
| Ounces | Grams | 28.4 |
| Grams | Ounces | 0.04 |

**Susan Niner Janes** is an American craft designer, author and editor living in England, and the author of *New Ideas in Ribboncraft* from North Light Books. She writes for adults and children on subjects ranging from fabric crafts and sewing to papercrafts, printing and rubber stamping. This is her eighth craft book. She is also a frequent contributor of projects for craft magazines. Her work has been featured in publications such as *Crafts Beautiful*, *Arts & Crafts* and *Prima*. Before moving to England, Susan was the assistant needlework and crafts editor for *Woman's World* magazine. As a Certified Professional Demonstrator, Susan creates sample projects for craft manufacturers and demonstrates crafts at consumer shows. She holds a degree in apparel design from Cornell University, New York.

# DEDICATION

For Leah and Daniel—two great kids.
Thanks for the positive parenting experience.
I love you guys.

— — — — — — — —

# ACKNOWLEDGMENTS

Many thanks to the friendly, gifted
and insightful North Light creative team.
It is a privilege to work with you.

Special thanks to my enthusiastic and helpful editor,
David Oeters, and to Tricia Waddell, Christine Doyle,
Jolie Roth and photographer Christine Polomsky.

Many thanks to my loving and supportive family.
You know why!

— — — — — — —

# TABLE OF CONTENTS

It's great to be a twenty-first century papercrafter, because the Golden Age of Papercrafting is here and now! Never before has such a fantastic selection of specialized papercraft products—both gadgets and materials—been available, offering exciting and limitless creative possibilities.

Thanks to the archival-quality, acid-free papers and adhesives devised for the making of memory albums, it is now possible to make keepsake projects which will last for many, many years. It's a papercraft revolution—one giant leap!

Scrapbookers are a dedicated bunch of crafters, always on the lookout for new ways to present their memory album pages. Because of them, many innovative papercraft products have been introduced: paper-cutting equipment, paper punches in all shapes and sizes, paper edgers and corner rounders, and tools and templates for cutting out paper shapes. Other developments include machines for bonding and laminating papers and acid-free papers in an inspirational array of patterns, colors and textures.

If you are a devoted scrapbooker, then you are almost certainly accumulating an ever-growing collection of gadgets. You probably have a stash of decorative papers in search of a project. You may have been searching for any other craft applications for these marvelous tools and materials—not to mention your considerable papercraft skills—besides the making of memory albums. Look no further. This book is packed with useful ideas that reach beyond the confines of the two-dimensional album page.

You don't have to be a scrapbooker to create these projects. This book will update and fine-tune your skills, introducing you to the current crop of papercraft innovations.

Learning how to use the new generation of papercraft products will bring a new dimension—literally and figuratively—to how you approach papercrafting. You'll bubble over with creative ideas of your own, eagerly anticipating future papercraft innovations and trends.

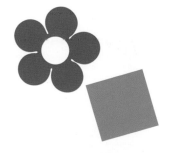

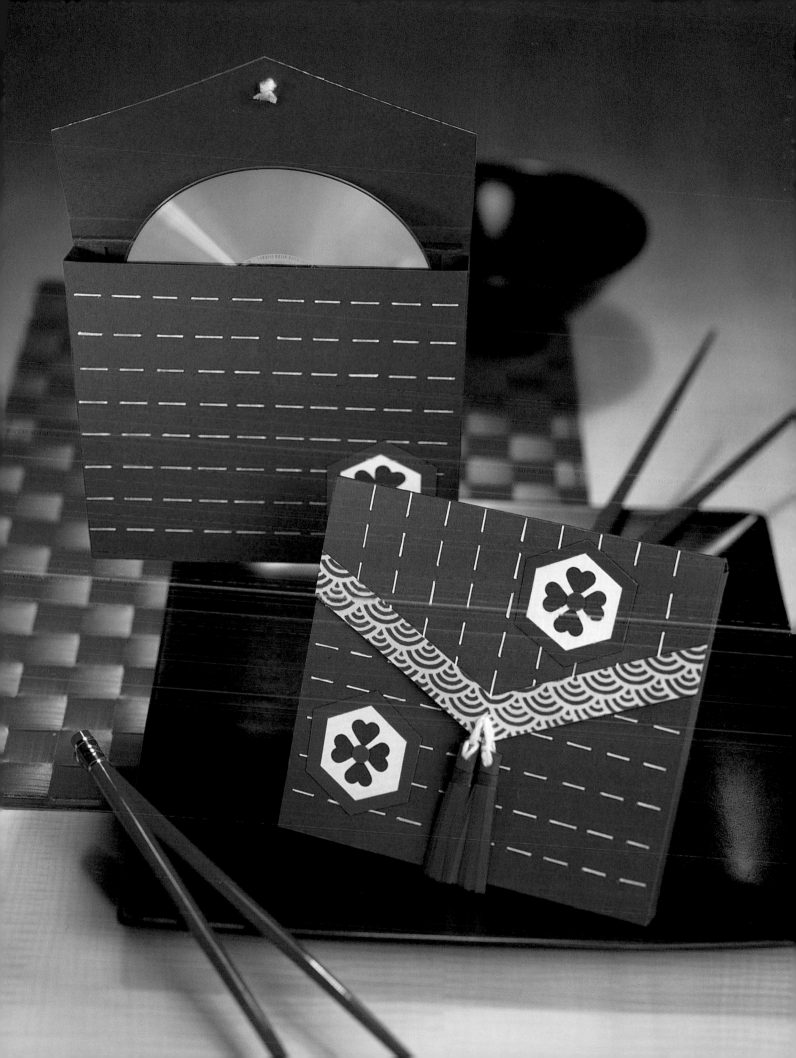

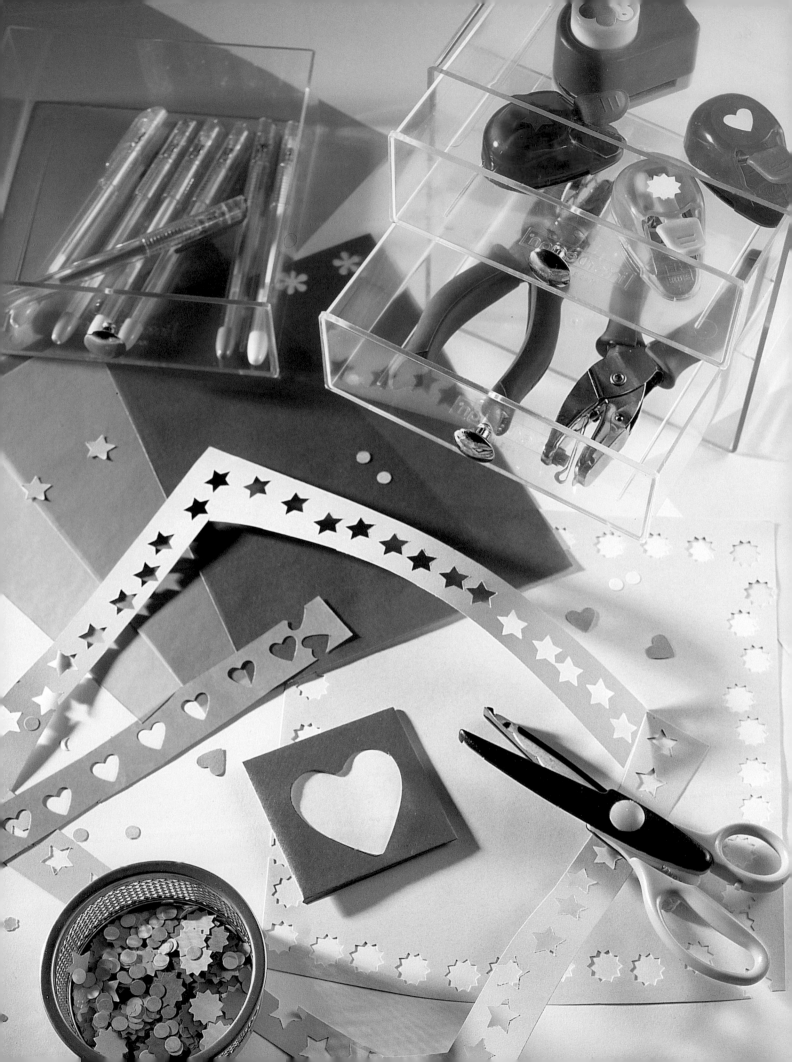

# Getting Started

Whenever I go to a scrapbooking or hobby store, I am faced with the dazzling array of paper in rainbow colors and the amazing selection of papercraft tools on display. If you are new to papercrafting, you might just be a bit overwhelmed or a little confused by the sheer volume of what's available to buy. The bottom line is this: papercraft is mostly about cutting paper—and most papercraft tools are mechanical devices for doing exactly that. Simple, really.

Some papercraft tools, like a craft knife—which is really just a razor blade on a stick—are pretty basic. Others, like a ShapeCutter, are sophisticated, state-of-the-art feats of engineering smarts. What it boils down to is this—they are different methods of cutting paper. The trick is knowing which gadget is right for the job at hand.

The old adage "a good craftsman knows his tools" holds true for paper-crafting. The good news is that getting acquainted with your papercraft tools is fun! You can learn the basics in minutes. As always, practice makes perfect. As you get to know your tools and their capabilities, you'll expand your creative repertoire. For instance, once you master paper edgers, you'll progress from using them exclusively for trimming paper edges to fashioning paper chains and more.

Familiarity with what your papercraft gadgets can do will leave you bursting with ideas and the delightful knowledge that if you have a papercraft tool kit and a stash of paper, a finished project is just minutes away.

The following pages give you some basic information and tips about paper-craft materials, techniques and equipment—what you need to get started and how to get the most out of them.

# MATERIALS

## Paper Primer

**Paper Primer** Variety of choice makes papercrafting a joy. Some papers don't even look like paper. For instance, they can be fabric-like or have metallic finishes. Whatever the paper, it is usually easy to cut and glue—in my opinion, it's the perfect handicraft material.

Here's a brief rundown of some of the papers you are likely to use in your crafting:

**SCRAPBOOKING PAPER AND CARDSTOCK:** Acid-free, archival-quality paper, created for use in memory albums. Cardstock is a heavier paper. Since scrapbooking paper is specially manufactured to minimize deterioration over time, it is ideal for keepsake projects. Scrapbooking papers come in a fantastic array of printed patterns and solids. Some of the designs are themed for special occasions. Double-sided patterns are often available. Scrapbooking vellums—that is, translucent papers—are also available. Standard sizes are 8½" × 11" (22cm × 28cm) or 12" × 12" (30cm × 30cm). The latter size is the standard measurement of a scrapbook page.

**CORRUGATED CARDBOARD:** Has a textured finish. Most familiar is fluted, which has tube-like ridges. You can buy corrugated paper in fine flute or coarse flute to suit your project. Other textured patterns include waves and basket weave.

**EMBOSSED PAPER:** Has raised surface designs.

**GIFT WRAP:** Ideal for papercraft projects with a limited life span. It is inexpensive; you can find it everywhere; there's an incredible choice of patterns, colors and finishes; and its wider width often comes in handy.

**HANDMADE PAPER:** Often softer and more fabric-like than machine-made paper. It may include plant matter for a natural-look decorative effect.

**MIRROR CARDSTOCK:** Has a high-gloss metallic finish. It comes in silver, gold and jewel-bright colors. Ideal for festive occasions.

**ORIGAMI PAPER:** Not just for folding! It comes in plain, reversible and printed varieties. Washi paper is a bit thicker and comes in larger sheets.

**PEARLESCENT PAPER:** Has a luxurious, shimmery, iridescent finish.

## TIP

*Clip sheets of paper onto a clothes hanger for convenient storage. This method is especially good for oversize sheets of paper that would be difficult to store flat.*

# Adhesives and Supplies

When choosing adhesives, you must consider the end use of your project. For short-use projects, use ordinary, everyday adhesives. For keepsake projects, use archival-quality adhesives (from a scrapbooking supplier). Always read the label to know how to best use your adhesive.

Keep all the following items in your craft box. These are the supplies you will find yourself turning to again and again while papercrafting.

**CRAFTER'S GLUE:** The familiar white general-purpose craft glue. It dries clear.

**DRY GLUE STICK:** Rub-on stick glue for bonding paper to paper. Particularly good when large, smooth expanses are needed.

**MASKING TAPE:** For joining two surfaces temporarily during crafting. Drafting tape is a special low-tack tape that won't tear delicate papers.

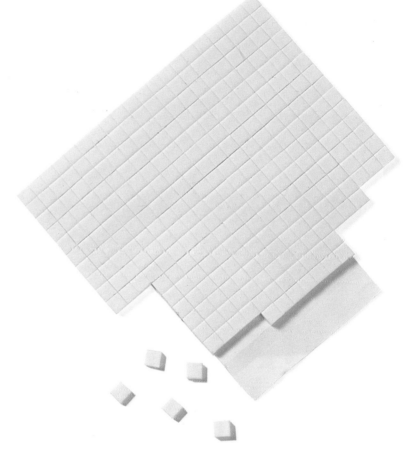

**TOOTHPICKS:** The ideal papercraft glue applicator. A toothpick helps get into tight corners and aids in applying glue sparingly.

**KNEADED ERASER:** Removes pencil marks from projects without leaving a crumbly residue.

**3-D DÉCOUPAGE SELF-ADHESIVE FOAM PADS:** For sticking paper together quickly when you want to give dimensional "lift" to a project.

# EQUIPMENT

**Papercraft Gadgets and Equipment** There are many tools for cutting, shaping and texturizing paper, including some absolutely genius gadgets and gizmos. Some papercrafting tools are essential, others less so—but all are fun and easy to use.

In this book, when a project calls for a specific papercraft tool, an effort has been made to suggest an alternative product whenever possible—because there's nearly always more than one way to get the job done.

The starred items on the following list are craft-kit essentials:

**CIRCLE CUTTER:** An adjustable, compass-like tool with a knife blade for cutting paper circles.

**\*CRAFT KNIFE:** The most essential papercraft tool. A razor-sharp blade mounted in a handle, a craft knife gives a cleaner, more precise cut than scissors. It should be used with a self-healing cutting mat.

**CORNER EDGERS:** Special scissors for cutting decorative corners on paper and cardstock.

**GEL PENS:** Can be used for writing on light or dark colors. The inks flow on easily and come in a good range of colors.

**MARKERS:** Metallic markers can add a festive touch to special projects (be safe and make sure you choose non-toxic inks).

**METAL RULER:** For measuring and cutting out your paper crafts. When using a craft knife, you lean it against a metal straightedge in order to cut perfect straight lines. It is useful to have metal rulers in several sizes: 6" (15cm), 12" (30cm) and either 18" (46cm) or 24" (61cm) are recommended.

**PAPER CRIMPER:** A tool that texturizes plain paper by pressing it between two embossed rollers. The most common patterns are ridges or waves.

**PAPER EDGERS:** Papercraft scissors with patterned blades. Paper edgers can be used for cutting fancy edges and making paper chains. An amazing variety of blade patterns are available. Basic shapes are pinking (zigzag) and scallops.

**PAPER PUNCHES:** Gadgets for die-cutting shapes out of paper. They come in two varieties: press-action punches for larger shapes—usually 1/2" (13mm) and larger—and hand punches, handheld squeeze-action punches for punching smaller shapes.

**\*RIGHT TRIANGLE:** A 45° right triangle is handy for checking whether your measured corners are truly perpendicular. Get into the habit of using one.

**\*SCISSORS:** Every papercrafter should have several different pairs of scissors kept expressly for papercrafting. Using scissors for other purposes would dull the blades. Small scissors are indispensable for delicate cutting. Use embroidery scissors or nail scissors. Curved nail scissors are good on curves. Handicraft scissors are blunt ended and smallish—about 5" (13cm) long. They are great for general craft use, such as trimming and coarse cutting.

**\*SELF-HEALING CUTTING MAT:** Use as your cutting surface in conjunction with a craft knife. The mat protects the tabletop and has a resilience that makes cutting easier.

**SHAPE CUTTER:** The Fiskars ShapeCutter is a tool in which a swivel blade is suspended in a carriage. It can be used with stencil templates to cut out decorative paper shapes. Another method of cutting shapes out uniformly is to use a system of nested templates, such as the Coluzzle Cutting System. This comes with a special handheld swivel knife and cutting mat.

**STENCIL KNIFE:** A variety of craft knife that has two parallel blades. The blades produce a line of uniform width.

**TRACING PAPER:** Keep a roll handy for making pattern tracings. Thumbnail sketch paper is a less expensive alternative.

**TWEEZERS:** Can be useful for picking up and positioning small punched paper shapes. Choose straight-tip or angled-tip—not pointy ones.

**XYRON MACHINE:** This mechanically laminates, applies adhesive to bond paper together, and makes magnets and stickers. The device has different cartridges for each purpose.

## TIP

*Papercraft tools are easy to use, but it's always a good idea to familiarize yourself with them before starting a project.*

# Where to Find Papercraft Supplies

Try hobby superstores, scrapbooking stores and your local art supply store first when looking for papercraft materials and equipment.

Toy stores can be unexpected treasure troves. They can be sources of paper edgers and fun papers, such as metallics and origami paper. Consumer craft shows are often showcases for new products and hard-to-find items. The Internet can also be a fabulous resource for the papercrafter. You can find whatever you need and order it by E-mail. Check out the resource directory at the back of this book for some useful Web sites.

Finally, a browse through the classified section of your favorite craft magazine is likely to yield useful mail-order shopping leads.

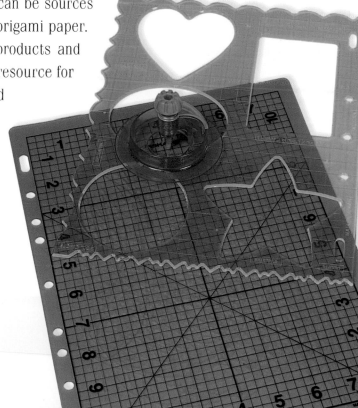

**Impressing a Pattern** Impressing a pattern outline using a stylus is a convenient way to transfer pattern markings onto paper. Impressing takes a lot less time than tracing because you don't have to go over the pattern outlines in pencil on the back of the design before transferring the design onto the project paper. Unlike tracing, there are no pencil lines to erase when the project is completed.

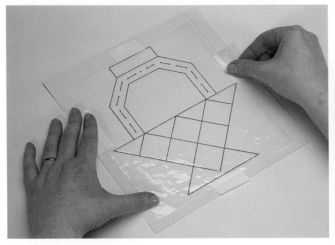

**1. TAPE THE PATTERN IN PLACE**

Enlarge or reduce the pattern on a photocopier until it is the correct size. Pencil-trace the pattern onto a piece of tracing paper. Tape the tracing onto the piece of decorative paper you have selected for the project.

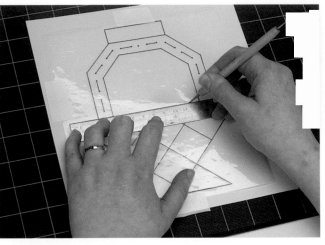

**2. IMPRESS THE PATTERN**

Place the taped pattern on a mat or a piece of scrap cardstock—not a hard surface. Use a stylus to impress the pattern into the paper. A metal ruler can help you keep the lines straight. A dry fine-point pen makes an excellent stylus. You can also use an embossing tool.

## TIP

If you are going to use the pattern tracing several times, it is a good idea to reinforce it by applying a layer of clear, self-adhesive vinyl, such as book-covering material. This will make it durable for repeated use.

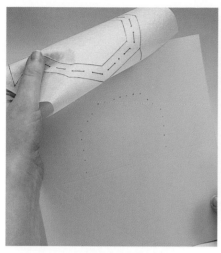

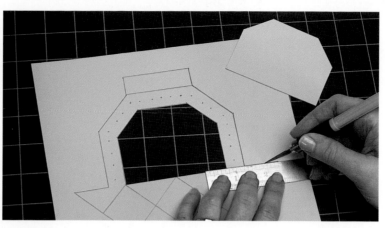

## 3. UNCOVER THE IMPRESSED PATTERN

Untape the pattern tracing to reveal the impressed lines. If the lines are hard to see, trace over them lightly with a pencil. On a dark surface, you may wish to outline the design in white gel pen—but only if the outlines will not be visible in the finished project, because the ink is permanent.

## 4. CUT OUT THE SHAPE

Use a craft knife and cut out the shape. Use a ruler to keep the lines straight. Always cut over a self-healing cutting mat. Use a fresh, sharp blade in the craft knife. It is time to change blades when the knife starts to drag on the paper. For cutting curves, you may find it easier to use small scissors, such as embroidery or nail scissors. Keep these expressly for paper use to prevent the blades from dulling.

# Scoring In order to fold thicker papers and cardstock smoothly, you must first score the paper; that is, partially cut through it.

**TIP**

Practice scoring on a test piece of the project paper. See if it is better to score on the inside or the outside of the paper. You'll know which side is right by how easily the paper folds. If you mistakenly cut too deeply, position a piece of cellophane tape behind the cut to mend the paper and salvage the project.

## 1. SCORING

Swipe the craft knife lightly across the paper, taking extra care not to cut too deeply. Lean the knife against a metal straightedge to score a perfect straight line.

## 2. FOLDING

Fold along the scored line. Use your thumbnail to crease a nice, crisp fold.

# Using Paper Punches
An enthusiastic papercrafter (that's the only kind!) will soon build up a sizeable collection of paper punches.

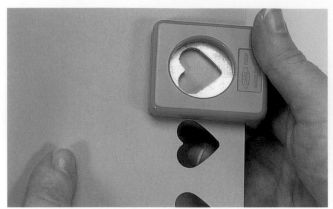

UPSIDE-DOWN PLACEMENT
--------------------------

If you hold your punch upside down, you can view through the "window," so you can position your punch precisely where you want it on the paper. Some punches have alignment notches on the casing to assist in placement. Mark a pencil dot at each notch, then match up the dot with the notch to place the adjacent cutout.

PUNCH MAINTENANCE
--------------------

You can sharpen the punch by punching through a piece of aluminum foil several times. If your paper punch starts to stick, lubricate it by punching through a piece of waxed paper a few times.

# Using Hand Punches
Another type of paper punch is the handheld squeeze-action punch. Hand punches are used for punching smaller shapes in quick succession.

🌸 Tweezers are great for picking up and positioning tiny punched shapes.

🌸 When making a border of hand-punched shapes, measure and mark punch positions on the back of the paper. For perfect alignment, draw a straight guideline, then make pencil dots along it at positions where the center of each punched shape should be located.

🌸 Some hand punches have a built-in "confetti catcher"—a compartment that collects the punched shapes. Remember to empty it periodically by swinging open the "trap door." Save the confetti, it might come in handy for future papercraft projects.

The "confetti catcher" is an excellent source of confetti and extra punched shapes.

# Cutting Shapes

The Fiskars ShapeCutter is a system for making paper cutouts. It consists of the ShapeCutter tool—a cutting blade suspended in a circular carriage, so it can swivel freely; a plastic template with stencils for making the cutout shapes; and a self-healing cutting mat. A large selection of ShapeTemplates is available for making shapes in various sizes. Themed templates are also available. The ShapeCutter can also be used for freehand cutting, but the projects in this book use it only for template cutting.

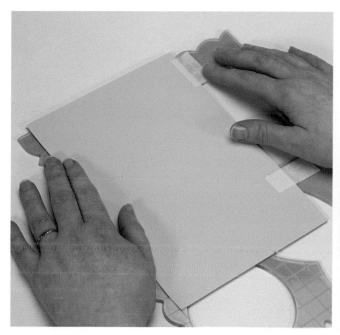

### 1. TAPE THE PAPER

Tape the paper onto the back of the template, so it doesn't shift during cutting. The smooth side of the template is the front, and the raised grid lines are on the back.

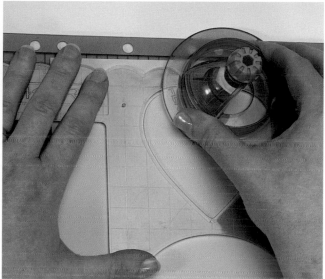

### 2. USE THE SHAPECUTTER

Hold the ShapeCutter by the textured outside ring, then slide it along the edge of the template. Start cutting at a straight side of the shape and align the blade parallel to the edge of the template. Slow down as you go around corners or extreme curves. If the cutter is not producing smooth edges, then it's time to replace the blade.

## TIP

*You may have to adjust the blade depth to suit the thickness of the cardstock. For cutting with a template, twist the orange knob clockwise to lower the blade and counter-clockwise to raise it. Do a test run on a scrap of the paper you intend to use before you cut out your project "for real."*

# Using Paper Edgers

Paper edgers are a craft innovation that has caught on like wildfire. It's easy to see why: they're so much fun! Paper edgers are scissors with specially shaped blades that can cut paper edges in decorative patterns. They come in an amazing variety of blade patterns.

❀ In order to make the edged pattern continuous, you must realign the blades with every cut. After making your cut, advance the blade, at the same time matching it with the shapes on the cut paper edge.

❀ Each paper edger blade pattern has its own "feel." Get used to handling each design. Practice on scrap paper, especially the tricky bits, like negotiating curves and corners. More intricate designs require greater pressure while cutting.

❀ To cut a straight paper-edged line, rule a pencil line on the back of the paper, then cut against it.

❀ Save time by using straight scissors to cut the project out and then remove excess paper. Use paper edgers for the fancy trimming, after the basic shape has been cut out.

❀ When cutting a double-edged strip of paper, you must reverse the direction of the strip to cut the second side. (Or, you can fold the paper in half lengthwise and cut both edges simultaneously—but this method will leave a center crease.)

❀ Use specially designed corner edgers for a one-snip corner treatment.

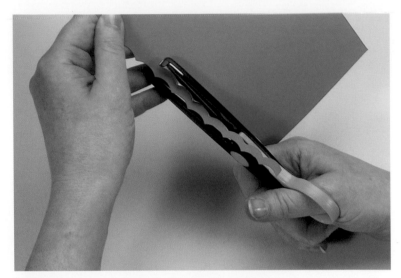

Advance your blade each time you make a cut to keep the pattern continuous.

Use a pencil line to keep your cuts straight, and trim away excess paper before you begin.

# Crimping Paper

Paper crimping allows you to incorporate an element of texture to a project. Texture can be an exciting and beautiful addition to any papercrafted project. Normally you would have to find the right textured paper to fit your project, but with a paper crimper it is easy to texturize plain paper. Corrugated ridges are the most common roller pattern. Insert the paper between the two ridged rollers. Squeeze the handles together tightly with one hand; this secures the paper. With your other hand, turn the key to advance the paper through the rollers. Once you master the basic techniques, experiment to find new ways to bring texture to your project using a paper crimper.

Check to make sure the paper goes through the rollers evenly.

❁ To keep your paper correctly aligned, tape a piece of masking tape onto the center of the paper support bar (in front of the rollers). This mark will help you keep the center of the paper lined up. As you feed the paper through the rollers, check the tape to see if any adjustment is required. Straighten the paper gradually, if necessary.

❁ To create a waffle effect, run the paper through the crimpers twice. Make a second pass perpendicular to the first one.

❁ Make sure your paper is narrower than the crimper width. This sounds obvious, but mistakes can happen, especially if you pass the paper through the crimper a second time in another direction.

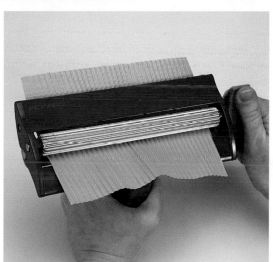

To create a waffle effect, put the paper through a second time, perpendicular to the first.

# Papercrafting Projects

Back in the "Swinging '60s," paper dresses were made up as novelty items. A wacky idea, yes, but it does illustrate just what a versatile material paper is. In fact, you can make surprisingly more out of paper than the usual stuff that comes to mind because there are all sorts of innovative developments in both paper and papercrafting tools to take advantage of. It is my hope that the projects in this book offer some refreshingly different papercrafted creations in a range of categories including greeting cards, giftwrap ideas, ornaments, and home decorating accents. The projects are pretty, practical and fun.

This book is filled with exciting papercraft projects, such as handmade greeting cards. It's always a pleasant surprise to receive a handmade greeting card instead of a mass-produced one. With the help of the latest papercraft gadgets, such as paper punches and paper edgers, your cards can have a professional appearance. Not only will your handiwork earn keepsake status—it's likely to be put on permanent display.

But you'll find so much more on these pages. When you think of home decorating accessories, paper items may not immediately spring to mind. Think just a little harder, and—yes, paper homewares have always been there, doing what they do best—brightening things up colorfully and inexpensively. They are time-tested favorites re-invented to look fresh and new.

Every project in this book has a charm and personality, and I hope you have as much fun making them as I did presenting them to you.

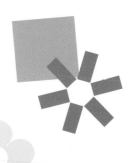

## ⭐ MATERIALS LIST

### PAPER

One 8½" × 11" (22cm × 28cm) piece of marble-look cardstock, in beige

One 8½" × 11" (22cm × 28cm) piece of parchment-look cardstock, in light blue

Elephant hide paper: 1 sheet each of tan, dark blue, terra-cotta, light green and dark green

A scrap of natural-colored corrugated cardboard

### ADDITIONAL SUPPLIES

Clear cellophane

Dry glue stick

Crafter's glue

Toothpicks

Kneaded eraser

Pencil

Craft knife

Self-healing cutting mat

Paper punches: diamond, leaf with stem, five-petal flower

Paper edgers: clouds

Metal ruler

Small scissors

Hand punch: ⅛" (3mm) circle

# terrarium card

**T**his card is a papercraft gadget interpretation of a fun 1970s pastime, sand-painting. Part of sand-painting's ongoing appeal is the "how'd you do that?" mystery factor. Well, the very same can be said of this papercrafted greeting card! It looks tricky to do—but appearances are deceiving!

Instead of sprinkling, poking and prodding grains of colored sand to build up patterns, paper "sand-painting" is crafted using glued cutouts—squiggly paper strips cut using decorative edgers—plus paper-punched shapes. "Elephant hide" paper, which has a grainy appearance, is ideal for creating a sand-like effect. The card has a top fold, so you can easily prop it up to display your handiwork!

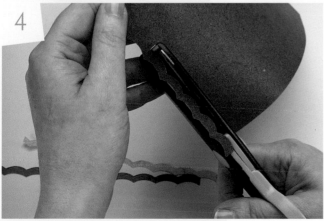

### 1. TRACE AND CUT OUT THE CARD

Enlarge the pattern, given on page 27. Trace it onto a piece of beige cardstock for a top fold card. Lightly score the fold. Cut out the terrarium bottle shape from the card front.

### 2. TRACE TERRARIUM SHAPE ONTO THE BACKING PAPER

Cut a piece of blue cardstock exactly the size of the card front. Cut a piece of tan elephant hide (for the "soil") 2¾" (7cm) high by the width of the blue cardstock. Glue the tan paper onto the bottom of the cardstock using a dry glue stick, and lay the terrarium cutout directly over the two-tone backing card. Pencil the terrarium outline onto the backing card.

### 3. ADD THE DARK BLUE CUTOUTS

Cut a 1¾" (45mm) strip of dark blue paper and glue it onto the bottom of the backing card, overlapping the tan elephant hide. Also from dark blue, punch five diamond shapes. Glue a row of horizontal diamonds just above the dark blue strip.

### 4. CUT THE SCALLOP BANDS

Using the cloud paper edgers, cut the scallop bands from light green, dark green, and terra cotta paper. To start, draw a baseline across the paper. Cut along the line, aligning scallop points with the line. Discard the paper below the baseline. Next, using the previous cut as your new baseline, cut across the paper, aligning scallop points. Cut the scallop band about ¼" (6mm) wide. Make all the bands in this way.

### 5. ADD FLOWER STEMS AND LEAVES

Glue the scalloped bands in place on the terrarium card using a dry glue stick. Use small scissors to cut the curved flower stems freehand. Glue the stems in place using crafter's glue applied with a toothpick. Punch out the leaves using a leaf-shaped paper punch. Glue the leaves onto the stems with crafter's glue.

### 6. ADD THE FLOWERS

Punch out three flowers and glue them in place using crafter's glue. Punch the flower centers with the ⅛" (3mm) circle punch and glue them in place. Next, remove the pencil outline using a kneaded eraser.

### 7. GLUE CELLOPHANE BEHIND THE WINDOW

Clear cellophane is used to create the appearance of a glass terrarium jar. Cut a piece of cellophane slightly larger than the terrarium cutout. On the back of the card front, apply a thin line of crafter's glue all around the cutout. Carefully smooth on the cellophane. Turn the card over. If any glue has crept onto the cellophane, clear it away with the tip of a toothpick or a moist tissue.

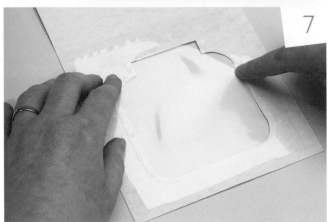

### 8. COMPLETE THE CARD

Glue the terrarium behind the cellophane window. Apply a line of crafter's glue across the top and bottom edges of the terrarium design and at the middle of each side. Position the terrarium behind the card front and smooth it in place. Finally, cut the terrarium "lid" out from corrugated cardboard and glue it onto the card front.

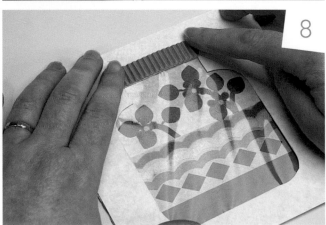

### Get the Edge

Vary your sand-painted designs! Besides scallops, other paper edger blade styles are appropriate for mock sand-painted effects. Notch, wavy, heartbeat, and corkscrew patterns work well. Also try other punch shapes; geometrics, such as triangles, are best.

## ✿ VARIATION IDEAS

Using this same basic format, you can create many more "sand-painted" pieces of art to give to friends and family! The use of different colored scalloped bands gives you a vastly different card. A variety of bottle shapes are available to you. Make up several bottles of different shapes and arrange them together for a striking presentation.

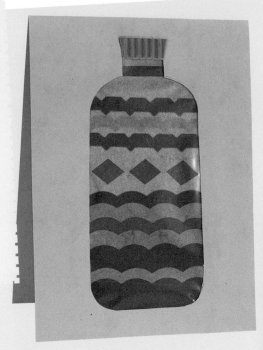

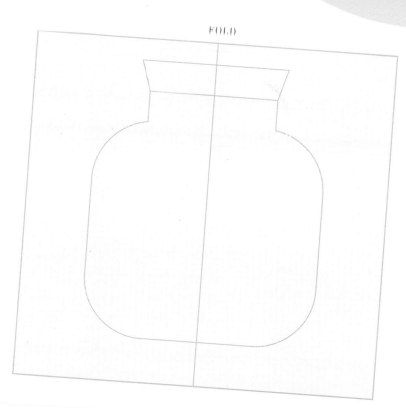

FOLD

Enlarge the pattern 143% for the front of the folded card.

⭐ **MATERIALS LIST**

**PAPER**

One 8½" × 11" (22cm × 28cm) sheet of cardstock in each of the following colors: navy blue, silver mirror and white (for reusable pattern template)

One 8½" × 11" (22cm × 28cm) sheet of vellum in each of the following colors: white pearlescent and dark blue

**ADDITIONAL SUPPLIES**

Clear cellophane

Crafter's glue

Toothpicks

Kneaded eraser

Pencil

Craft knife

Self-healing cutting mat

Metal ruler

Shape cutter

Shape template: shapes or circles

Hand punches: ¹⁄₁₆" (2mm) and ⅛" (3mm) circle

Paper punches: ½" (13mm) circle, ½" (13mm) star and ½" (13mm) spiral

# crystal ball card

This whimsical crystal ball card works real magic. It brings a smile to the face of whoever you send it to. Plus, it is as much fun to make as it is to receive. The card is suitable for a variety of occasions—as a good luck card, a Halloween card or a greeting for a fantasy buff.

The inspiration for this card is snow globe toys—those childhood favorites, most often acquired as stocking stuffers or souvenirs. Instead of swirling snowflakes, this card produces a cosmic shower of shooting stars!

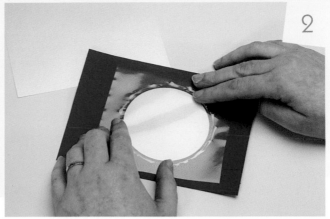

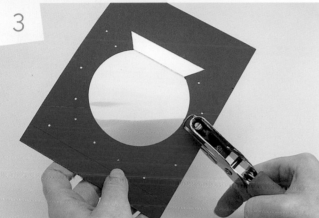

## 1. CUT OUT THE CARD
--------------------

Enlarge the card pattern, given on page 33. Using the card template, trace and cut out the greeting card front and back pieces from navy blue cardstock. Trace the globe pattern onto the card front (card front has the top fold). Lightly score the top fold using a craft knife and ruler. Next, cut the circle out using the shape cutter.

## 2. GLUE ON THE CELLOPHANE
-------------------------

Cut a piece of pearlescent white vellum the size of the card front. This will be the back of the snow globe. Trace the globe pattern in pencil in the center of the vellum. Cut a piece of clear cellophane to fit behind the circle cutout. On the back of the card, apply crafter's glue around the circle edges sparingly and carefully. Smooth the cellophane in place.

## 3. PREPARE THE CARD FRONT
-------------------------

Trace and cut out the globe base from mirror cardstock. Attach it to the bottom of the globe with crafter's glue. Next, use the $\frac{1}{16}$" (2mm) circle hand punch to add a few random holes around the globe. When held up to the light, these holes will be "distant twinkling stars." Add as many or as few holes as you like.

## 4. BEGIN THE CRESCENT MOON
--------------------------

Use the $\frac{1}{2}$" (13mm) circle punch to make a crescent moon. This is done in two steps. First, punch a semi-circle from the mirror cardstock. To do this, the punch must overlap the card edge, as shown.

### 5. COMPLETE THE CRESCENT MOON

Use the back of the punch so you can look through the cutout for easy placement. Position the circle over the previously punched arc. Punch out the shape to produce the crescent moon.

### 6. DECORATE THE CARD FRONT

Punch out several stars from mirror cardstock. Affix them to the card front with crafter's glue. Also glue on the crescent moon.

### 7. CUT OUT THE WAND

Cut out a 2½" (6cm) long by ¼" (6mm) wide strip of mirror card. Add a tip of pearlescent paper to the wand with crafter's glue. Glue the wand onto the bottom of the card.

**Recycled Artistry**

*If you've saved punch-outs from your other projects, you can use them in the cellophane globe! Keep your leftover punch-outs in a plastic bag, and use them for projects such as this that require extra punches.*

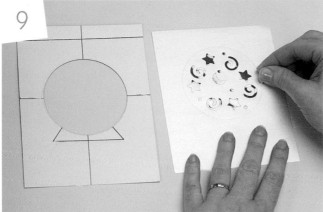

### 8. PUNCH OUT THE SNOW GLOBE CONFETTI

Use your paper punches to cut a variety of shapes for inside the globe. For this card, we used twenty-five blue vellum ½" (13mm) stars. From the mirror cardstock cut four ½" (13mm) spirals, four ½" (13mm) stars, one crescent moon (see steps 4–5, above) and seven ⅛" (3mm) punched circles.

### 9. GLUE MIRROR SHAPES INSIDE THE GLOBE

The penciled circle on the pearlescent vellum (see step 2) is your guide for gluing on the mirror cardstock embellishments. Inside the circle, glue on the mirror shapes with crafter's glue, arranging them as you wish them to appear on your completed card.

### 10. ASSEMBLE THE CARD FRONT

Flex the card front a few times. This eases the paper so the shapes can move around freely within the globe. Next, place the card front face down on your work surface. Place the blue vellum stars in the center of the cellophane. Apply glue around the edges of the circle. Smooth the pearlescent vellum onto the back of the card front, with the mirror shapes face down. Add a bit of glue to the corners of the pearlescent paper to affix it to the blue card front.

### 11. GLUE THE CARD TOGETHER

Crease the fold on the card front. Apply glue to the underside of the flap. Glue the flap onto the card back piece, as shown.

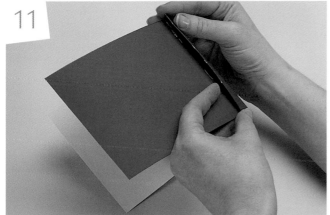

## ✿ VARIATION IDEA: STAR AND FLOWERS

Here's another quick-make idea. Use the shape cutter to cut out a star in the front of the card, then make a shimmery star to hang in the hole you've made. Front the star with a smaller, translucent card and stitch it in place with yarn. Fill the star with flower and circle confetti and glue more flowers and circles around the star for decoration. This card is sure to put a smile on someone's face!

## ✿ VARIATION IDEA: FISH POND

If you've made the crystal ball card, then crafting a fish pond is a cinch. Start with a shape cutter cutout, back it with colored translucent paper—and you've got the makings of a delightful papercrafted lily pond. Cut an oval pond shape, back with green vellum for the water, glue on punched paper water lilies and goldfish. Mount the hanging on your window using poster putty, or punch a hole at the top and add a ribbon hanging loop.

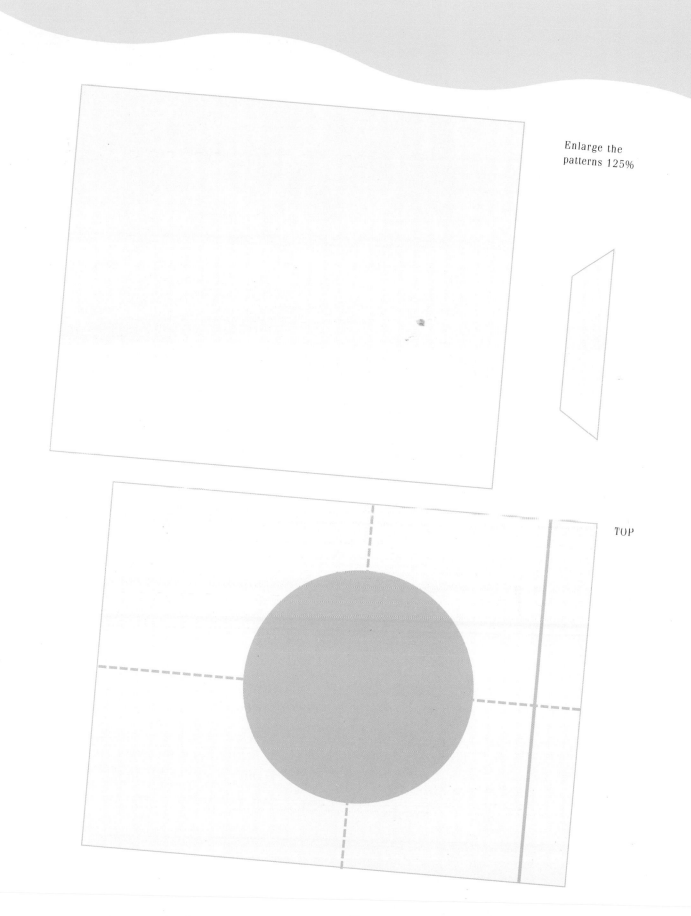

Enlarge the
patterns 125%

TOP

# mola card

**M**ola embroidery is a style of reverse appliqué unique to the Cuna Indians who live on the San Blas Islands off the coast of Panama. A typical Mola design depicts the spectacular wildlife and lush vegetation of the rain forest using bold shapes and a burst of vibrant tropical hues.

Creating Mola embroidery is a time-consuming process. In fact, a Mola panel takes hours and hours of labor-intensive needlework to create. The good news is that this card can be produced in well under an hour! Papercraft gadgets make easy work of the Mola design. A stencil cutter is used for the swirly slitted background pattern, while hand punches and decorative paper edgers also contribute to the finished effect—a papercrafted tropical paradise!

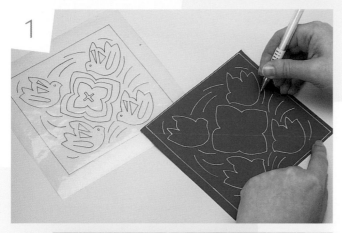

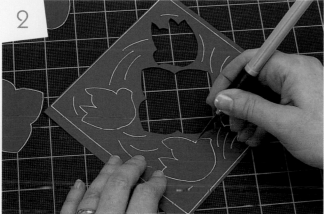

### 1. TRANSFER THE PATTERN

Enlarge the pattern given on page 39. Cut a piece of blue cardstock measuring 5½" (14cm) square. Tape the blue paper behind the pattern with masking tape. Use a stylus to impress the pattern outline onto the blue card. To see the outline more clearly, go over it with a white gel pen.

### 2. CUT OUT TWO DOVES AND THE FLOWER

Using the craft knife, cut out the upper right and lower left doves and the center flower. Make sure to cut just outside the white lines.

### 3. CUT THE DECORATIVE LINES

Using the stencil cutter, cut all the curved decorative lines that will be yellow in the finished design. Straddle the white lines as you cut, creating a line that is ⅛" (3mm) wide. A craft knife can be used as an alternative to a stencil cutter.

## Paper Chase

*Careful paper choice is crucial to the success of your Mola design. The distinctive feature of the Mola design is surface texture created by the cut away areas, so you want the depth of these to be noticeable. Choose cardstock thick enough to create a three-dimensional appearance, but thin enough to cut easily in double layers.*

### 4. REMOVE THE CARD STRIPS

Cut across the short ends of each stencil cut strip with a craft knife, then remove and discard the card strips. The flattened tail of the stencil cutter handle can be used to pick out the cut card strips.

### 5. PINK THE EDGES

With pinking pattern decorative edgers, trim the blue card. Keep scissors inside the marked white lines.

### 6. PREPARE THE YELLOW LAYER

Cut a piece of yellow card 6" (15cm) square. Mark a border ¼" (6mm) inside the card edges. Glue the blue cut out centered on top of the yellow square. To do this, apply crafter's glue onto the back of the blue card, gluing around the doves and the flower cut out. Apply glue sparingly with a toothpick. Also glue all four corners and the middle of each side. Next, with a stylus, transfer the outlines for the design elements that appear red. Go over the outlines in pencil.

## Speed Mola

*If you are in a hurry, then you can approximate the look of Mola embroidery using glued-on cardstock cutouts. You can still use the patterns provided—only build up layers of cut outs rather than removing them. Still use the stencil cutter to create the background pattern, but glue on the curved strips instead of cutting them away. The finished design will lack the three-dimensional interest of the cut-away version, but it will still get across the unique quality of Mola designs in terms of shape, color and subject matter.*

**TIP**

*Tweezers can be helpful for positioning small glued elements. Straight-tipped tweezers are preferable to pointy ones— much easier to pick up the cutouts!*

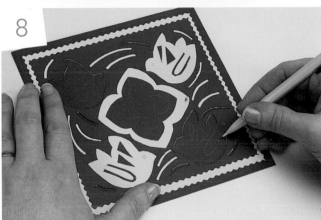

### 7. CUT OUT THE YELLOW LAYER

With the craft knife, cut out the design elements that will be red and the two remaining doves. Remember you are cutting through two layers of cardstock. Cut out the flower center, then cut out the cross and set it aside to glue on later. Cut out the decorative triangles on the yellow doves. With the stencil cutter, cut out the remaining curved decorative lines and the wings on the doves. Pink the edges of the card, as for Step 5. Place the yellow layer on the red card to check that you have cut out all the elements.

### 8. MARK THE RED LAYER

Cut a piece of red cardstock 6½" (17cm) square. Mark a ¼" (6mm) border. Glue the yellow card onto the red, taking care to glue around the cutouts and at the corners. Tape the pattern over the design and use the stylus to trace the parts that will be green. Remove the pattern.

### 9. CUT OUT THE RED LAYER

Use a craft knife to cut out the elements that will be green: the center flower and the triangles on the red doves. Use the stencil cutter to cut out the wings on the red doves. Pink the edges of the red card. Cut a piece of green cardstock measuring 6½" × 13" (17cm × 33cm). Score the middle of the card, then fold in half. Glue the red card onto the green card, centered, with the fold of the green card at the top.

### 10. COMPLETE THE CARD

Punch two green eyes and two red eyes with the ⅛" (3mm) circle punch. Also punch out seven small green flowers. Glue these punched shapes and the yellow cross onto the card as shown.

## ✿ VARIATION IDEA: DIFFERENT COLORS, DIFFERENT CARD!

You can use different colors of paper to make strikingly different cards using the same patterns and techniques presented here. And with so many paper styles to choose from, you will never run out of possibilities. The card below was made by adding punched paper pieces, rather than cutting them away, as a quick-make technique. The gift tag was a quick-make as well, and would be a fabulous addition to any gift presentation. Speed Mola! Enjoy!

## ✿ VARIATION IDEA: MOLA BOOKMARK

This is a simplified version of the card design, so if you know how to make the card, the bookmark's a breeze.

## Design Your Own Paper Mola

Think tropical rain forest for your subject matter and colors. (Wildlife: parrots, turtles, lizards. Color palette, rainbow: red, yellow, green, turquoise, magenta, orange.) Plan your design on paper (graph paper may help) using felt-tips to map out color areas. Keep it bold and simple. Start with a three-color design. (In authentic Molas, the top layer is often red.) Remember that you can "cheat" by including glued-on elements in addition to cutouts. In fact, authentic Molas often do include embroidered details and lettering. You can add "embroidery" to your design with gel pens. Simple lettering can be achieved using a scrapbooker's alphabet stencil.

Enlarge the pattern 125%. Dots (other than bird's eyes) show placement of punched flowers.

Enlarge the pattern 125%.

# new baby keepsake card

**W**elcome the new arrival with a sweet and simple baby-bib motif greeting card. Tucked inside the bib pocket is a papercraft replica of a soft toy. Handmade with TLC from archival-quality scrapbooking materials, this easy-make card is both a heartfelt greeting and a long-lasting commemorative gift. The top-fold design of the card makes it easy to stand up for display.

Fun-to-use papercraft gadgets make crafting this card a cinch. The waffle-like texture of the paper bib, crinkled with a paper crimper, is a dead ringer for piqué fabric. Paper punches and corner rounders speed up card construction. Happy birthday, little one!

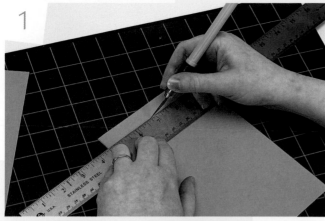

### 1. CUT OUT THE CARD
--------------------

The greeting card is made in two pieces, so that you can fit it onto standard-size scrapbooking cardstock, either 8½" × 11" (22cm × 28cm) or 12" × 12" (30cm × 30cm). Cut out the card pieces using a craft knife held against a metal ruler. Measure and cut out one 5" × 7" (13cm × 18cm) piece of card with a ⅝" (1.5cm) fold added across the top. Cut the card back piece exactly 5" × 7" (13cm × 18cm). On the card front piece, score the fold line to make creasing easier.

### 2. GLUE THE CARD TOGETHER
----------------------------

With the scored line face down, fold down the flap. Crease the fold with your fingernail for a nice, crisp edge. Apply crafter's glue to the inside of the flap. Glue the smaller piece of card on top of this, aligning the top of the card with the creased fold on the flap. The flap belongs on the back of the card. The writing surface is inside the greeting card, on the smaller piece of card.

### 3. CUT THE ROUNDED CORNERS
-----------------------------

Using the corner rounders, trim all four corners of the card. Open the rounders and slide the corner of the card underneath the guide slot until the paper is flush with the edges of the guide. Cut the corner, then repeat for the remaining three corners.

### 4. CRIMP THE BIB PAPER
---------------------

Cut out a piece of blue paper about 4½" × 6½" (11cm × 17cm). Insert it between the rollers of the crimper, making sure the top edge of the paper is parallel to the lines on the roller. Squeeze the crimper handle tightly to clamp the rollers together, then crank the key toward you to advance the paper and create the corrugated ridges.

### 5. CRIMP THE PAPER AGAIN

Turn the crimped paper 90° and insert the paper, held lengthwise, between the rollers. Pass the paper through the crimper a second time. This creates a waffle-like texture. Enlarge the bib pattern (see page 45) and cut it out in cardstock. Punch holes where marked on the pattern using a 1/16" (2mm) circle hand punch. Position the bib pattern over the waffle paper and trace around it with a pencil. Mark the holes for the ribbon, as well as the pocket fold.

### 6. CUT OUT THE BIB

Using the 1/16" (2mm) circle hand punch, punch out the holes as marked at the bib top and along the bottom edge. Cut out the curved neckline using scissors, and use a craft knife held against a metal ruler to cut out the remaining straight edges.

### 7. CUT THE ROUNDED CORNERS

Using a ruler to keep the edge straight, fold down the bib pocket. Using the corner rounders (see step 3), trim all four corners of the bib, including the pocket corners.

### 8. THREAD RIBBON THROUGH THE HOLES

Cut a 10" (25cm) piece of 1/8" (3mm) satin ribbon. Using a tapestry needle, thread the ribbon through the punched holes along the bib pocket edge. Sew an under-over running stitch. Make sure the ribbon doesn't twist. Cut the ends of the ribbon flush with the bib. Secure the ribbon ends with glue on the back of the pocket.

## TIP

The craft knife tends to catch on the crinkled paper. The best way to cut through it is to swipe the knife lightly several times across the paper until it makes a cut.

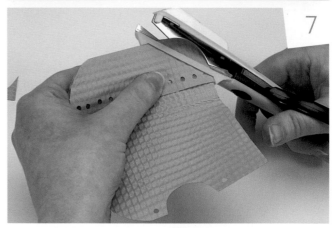

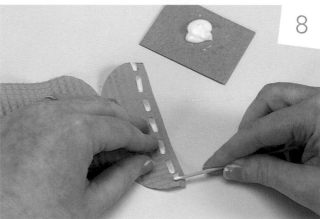

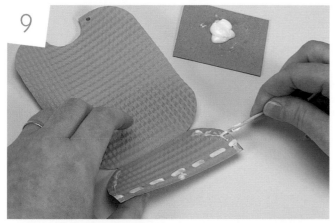

### 9. GLUE THE BIB POCKET

On the inside of the bib pocket, apply glue to the side edges. Also place a small dab of glue at the middle of the top edge. Fold the pocket up and gently tap the glued areas down.

### 10. PUNCH OUT THE DUCKS

Using the $1/16"$ (2mm) hand punch, punch five holes in the paper for the duck's eyes. Space the holes a bit more than a duck width apart. Turn the paper punch upside down so you can see exactly where to position the eye. Punch out five ducks.

### 11. GLUE THE DUCKS ONTO THE BIB POCKET

Glue the center duck first, then space the remaining ducks evenly across the pocket. All the ducks should face the same way.

### 12. ATTACH THE BIB TIES AND BOW

Cut two 8" (20cm) pieces of $1/8"$ (3mm) satin ribbon for the ties. Slip the end of one ribbon through the punched hole. On the back side of the bib, glue down the ribbon tail at a 45° angle. Repeat for the other ribbon. Tie the ribbons into a bow. Use scissors to trim the ribbon tails, then seal the ribbon ends with crafter's glue.

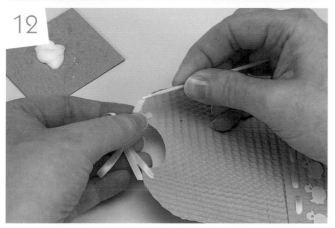

## Same Card, Different Looks

✳ To add background interest, make the greeting card out of patterned scrapbooking cardstock. Many adorable new baby motifs are available.

✳ Tuck a paper teddy into the bib pocket instead of a bunny.

✳ No paper crimper? Make the baby bib out of handmade paper. It has a fabric-like feel and appearance.

✳ For a refreshing change from the usual pink/blue baby color scheme, try alternative pastel colors such as peach, lilac or mint green. Very appealing!

### 13. GLUE THE BIB ONTO THE CARD

Apply glue sparingly to the back of the bib. Glue the bottom edge of the bib, behind the pocket. Also apply dabs of glue at the midpoint of each bib side and on the backs of the ribbon ties (at the bib top). Glue the bib onto the card front. Tap the bib in place gently to avoid smoothing out the crinkles. Finally, attach the bow knot with a dab of glue.

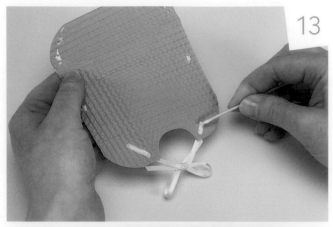

### 14. TRACE THE BUNNY

Trace the bunny pattern (see page 45) onto a small piece of pink cardstock (leftover from the card). Just make an impression of the bunny outline using a stylus, such as a dry fine-point pen. Go over the outline in pencil, if necessary. Use a gel pen to draw in the face of the bunny.

### 15. CUT OUT THE BUNNY

Use small scissors, such as embroidery or nail scissors. Cut on the inside of the pencil mark or the impressed outline, so the lines won't show on the completed cutout. Erase any lines left on the paper.

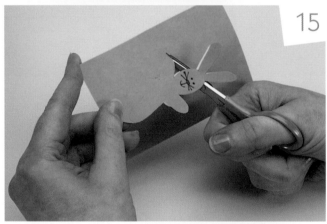

### 16. GLUE BOW ON BUNNY

Cut 3" (8cm) of ⅛" (3mm) ribbon for the bow. Tie a knot in the middle of the ribbon, trim the ends at an angle, then seal the ends as you did in step 12. Glue the bow onto the bunny and fold over one ear.

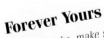

## Forever Yours

For a truly lasting keepsake, make sure all your card materials are of archival quality: paper, glue and ink—no halfway measures! You can find these supplies in a scrapbooking store or in the scrapbooking department of a hobby superstore. Sales staff will be happy to advise you.

### 17. PLACE THE BUNNY IN THE BIB POCKET

To finish the card, tuck the bunny into the bib pocket—there's no need to glue it down.

## Overcast Pocket Edges

*For a different look, overcast the edge of the bib pocket. You will need a 12" (30cm) piece of ribbon for this. Just sew the ribbon around and around over the pocket edge. For easier threading, use a 1/8" (3mm) hole punch for the stitching holes.*

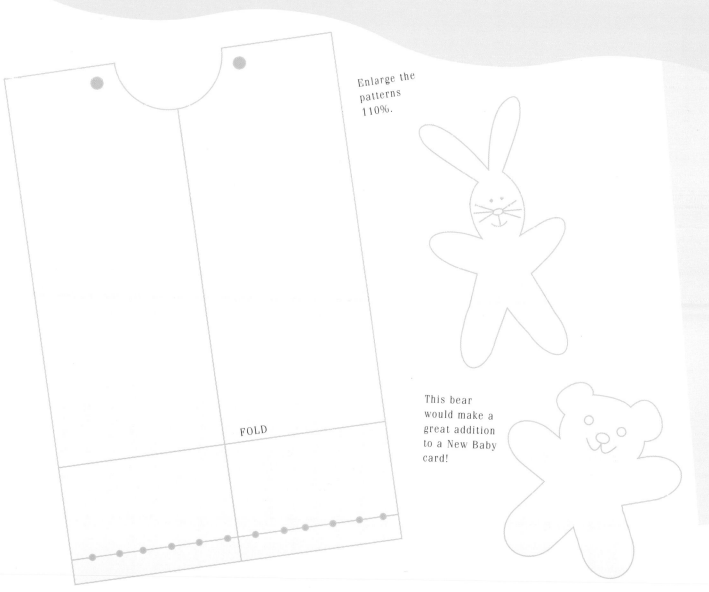

Enlarge the patterns 110%.

FOLD

This bear would make a great addition to a New Baby card!

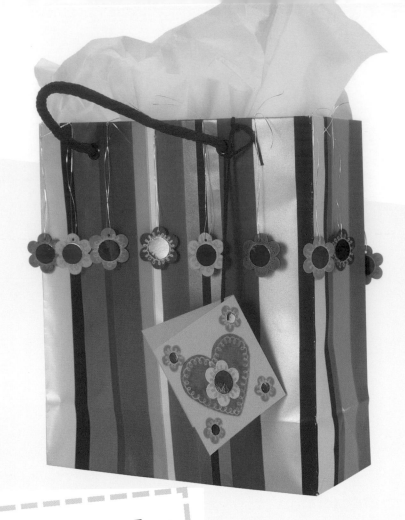

# shisha spangles gift bag & tag

**S**plashes of color and flashes of sparkle transform this gift bag and tag into a gorgeous "hippie chic" sensation. The spangles take their inspiration from the traditional shisha embroidery of India and Pakistan. A shisha is a mini mirror, usually a round one, which is appliquéd onto a background fabric using decorative buttonhole stitches.

We dressed up a purchased gift bag, but shisha spangles can also be used to make over other store bought articles, especially stationery items. Glue spangles onto school notebooks in decorative patterns, or use them to jazz up a pencil holder or other desktop articles. For another shisha-inspired project, turn to the shisha CD gift box on page 70.

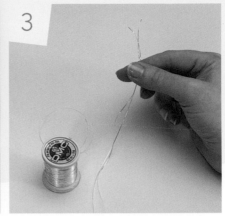

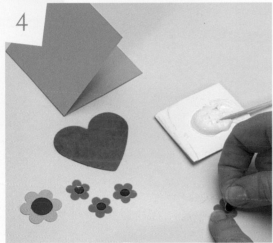

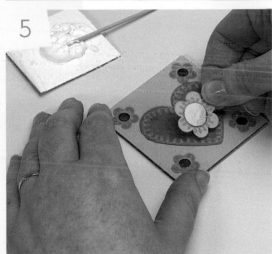

## 1. ASSEMBLE THE SPANGLE

Using the 1" (25mm) flower paper punch, make flowers out of brightly colored cardstock. Punch two $1/2$" (13mm) circles from mirrored cardstock for each flower that you punch. Using crafter's glue, affix a mirror circle to the center of each side of the flower.

## 2. DRAW A DESIGN

Use a gel pen to draw an embroidery-style design around the mirror circle. For example, a curlicue design is quick and easy to do. Use a gel pen color to contrast with the flower. Wait until the ink has dried, then decorate the flip side of the flower.

## 3. ADD THE SILVER THREAD

Punch a $1/16$" (2mm) hole in a petal of the spangle. Cut 12" (30cm) of silver thread and pass it through the hole in the spangle. Next, punch holes in the top of the gift bag for the spangles using the $1/16$" (2mm) punch; space the holes about $2^1/2$" (6cm) apart. Thread each spangle through a hole in the bag and knot it in place.

## 4. CUT OUT THE GIFT TAG

Cut out a rectangle of green cardstock measuring $2^1/2$" × 5" (6cm × 13cm). Score the cardstock and fold it in half. Next, cut out a pink 2" (5cm) heart, a 1" (25mm) flower and four $1/2$" (13mm) flowers. Then, cut out mirrored cardstock circles and glue them in place. You need a $1/2$" (13mm) circle for the larger flower and four $1/4$" (6mm) circles for the small flowers.

## 5. DECORATE AND ASSEMBLE THE TAG

Draw the embroidery designs around the mirrors and the heart, using a contrasting gel pen. Then glue the spangles and the heart onto the gift tag as shown. Punch a hole in the inside top left corner of the card. Cut about 12" (30cm) of burgundy embroidery thread and draw it through the hole. Tie the tag onto the gift bag handle.

## ⭐ MATERIALS LIST

### PAPER

One sheet of star-pattern gift wrap, lilac and silver

One sheet of heavy cardstock

Two pieces of mint green cardstock, $8^{1}/_{2}" \times 11"$ (22cm × 28cm)

Small piece of white pearlescent vellum

One piece of lightweight purple paper

### ADDITIONAL SUPPLIES

Matte embroidery cotton, purple

White self-adhesive mailing labels

Dry glue stick

Crafter's glue

Toothpicks

Pencil

Masking tape

Stylus

Circle cutter (compass-style)

Shape cutter

Shape template: stars

Craft knife

Self-healing cutting mat

Hand punch: $^{1}/_{8}"$ (3mm) circle

Metal ruler

# star gift box

This five-sided gift box looks all starry, cosmic and other-worldly—really snazzy packaging for that special birthday surprise!

Hard to believe, but the gift box starts out as just two circles of cardstock! This is good news because it means you'll never be without a gift box as long as you have a couple of pieces of cardstock, a shape cutter tool and a few minutes to spare!

To get from flat circles to three-dimensional box, you just fold in the curved side flaps, join the top and bottom box layers, and the box takes shape. This sort of box is called a pillow box, because it plumps up like a fluffy pillow.

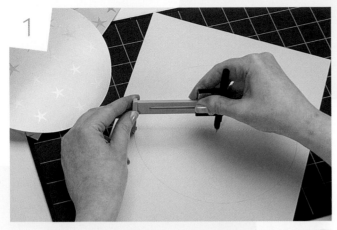

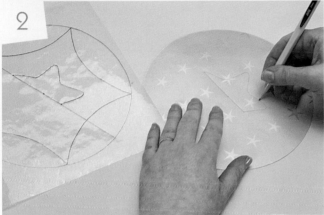

### 1. CUT OUT THE PAPER

Glue a piece of gift wrap onto a sheet of heavy cardstock with a dry glue stick. (Alternatively, a Xyron machine can be used to bond the gift wrap to the cardstock.) Using the compass cutter, cut out a 3½" (9cm) radius circle from the gift-wrap-covered cardstock. Cut out another 3½" (9cm) radius circle from plain green cardstock.

### 2. TRANSFER THE PATTERN MARKINGS

Make a tracing of the gift box pattern on page 53. Tape the tracing over the plain side of the gift wrap circle. Transfer the pattern outlines by pressing firmly with a stylus. Mark half a star in the middle of the circle, and the five curved side folds. On the plain cardstock circle, mark only the curved folds.

### 3. SHAPE-CUT THE STAR

Use the 3" (8cm) star on the shape template. Since you will be using only half of the star, begin cutting at the top point of the star, continue downward to the bottom point, then stop cutting! (For more detailed shape cutter how-tos, see page 19.)

## Pick a Patterned Paper

*To save time, make your gift box out of printed cardstock instead of gift wrap glued onto cardstock. Many fabulous scrapbooking papers can be found, some with double-sided designs. Reversible paper will work fabulously for the fold-back window cutout!*

### 4. SCORE THE STAR FOLD

On the back of the circle, lightly score the fold line of the star. Turn the circle gift wrap side up, then fold the star back.

### 5. SCORE THE CURVED FOLDS

On the back of the circle, score the curved folds. Do the same thing on the second cardstock circle.

### 6. GLUE THE TRANSLUCENT PAPER

Cut a small piece of pearlescent vellum to fit behind the star opening. Use a toothpick to apply crafter's glue sparingly around the opening. Smooth the paper in place, making sure there are no folds.

### 7. MAKE THE GIFT TAG

Use the shape cutter to make two 3" (8cm) stars. Cut one star from green cardstock and the other from lightweight purple paper. Fold the purple star in half and use a dry glue stick to affix half the purple star to the green star, with star points matching.

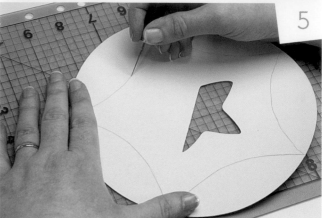

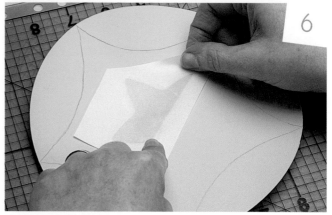

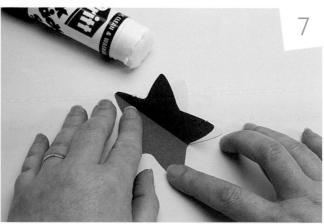

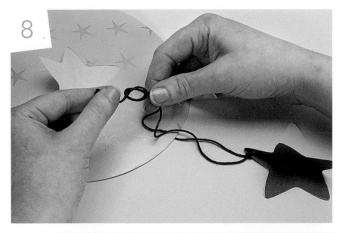

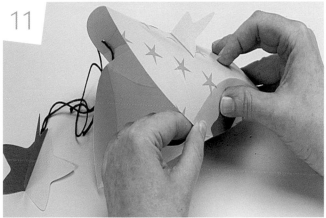

## TIP

*Use a piece of cellophane tape to hold the box flaps together, then position the sticker over this.*

### 8. ATTACH THE GIFT TAG

Cut 18" (46cm) of purple matte embroidery cotton. Use the 1/8" (3mm) hole punch to make a hole near the edge of the gift tag and another hole near the corner of a side flap. Tie the thread through the holes and knot to secure.

### 9. PREPARE THE BOX FOR ASSEMBLY

Use the shape cutter to make five 1 1/2" (38mm) star-shaped stickers. To make the sticker material, use a dry glue stick to bond a piece of purple paper onto a self-adhesive mailing label. Next, crease the scored, curved edges on both the gift wrap and plain circles.

### 10. ASSEMBLE THE BOX

Hold the folded circles with insides facing, edges even, and curved flaps matching. Fold the top flaps over the bottom flaps one at a time, and seal the bottom edge of each flap with a star sticker.

### 11. FINISH THE BOX

Do not seal all the flaps; leave two sides open. Place the present inside the box, then fold down and seal the two remaining flaps.

❀ VARIATION IDEAS

By simply changing the folds and the shape of the template, you can have an endless variety of gift boxes!

## What You See Is What You Get

*For our gift box, frosted vellum was used behind the star-shaped window opening. This is because we wanted the box contents to remain a mystery. However, if you are packaging food treats— such as candy or cookies—then back the window with clear cellophane to show off the yummy box contents!*

*Instead of a fold-back window, cut out the entire star shape, to give a better view of the goodies.*

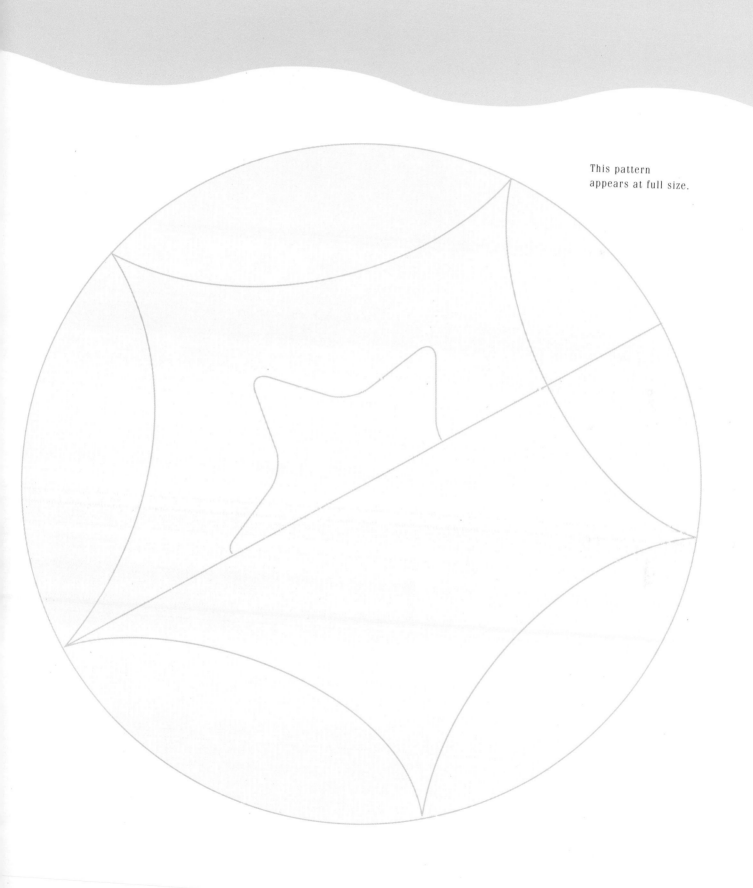

This pattern appears at full size.

**PAPER**

One sheet of yellow
pearlescent paper

Small pieces of the following
papers: patterned washi
or Origami paper, yellow
pearlescent card stock,
red pearlescent paper,
matte gold paper

**ADDITIONAL SUPPLIES**

Two self-adhesive mailing labels

12" (30cm) of gold cord

Dry glue stick

Crafter's glue (optional)

Pencil

Metallic gold marker (fine-point)

Scissors

Craft knife

Self-healing cutting mat

Metal ruler

Paper punch: 1" (25mm) six-petal
flower

Hand punches: $^1/_{16}$" (2mm) circle,
$^1/_4$" (6mm) circle

# japanese-style gift bag & tag

This attractive gift bag is quickly and easily made from just a single piece of paper, plus a few trimmings. Once you know how to make the bag, you can make it in different sizes, so you'll never, ever be without a gift wrap solution.

The bag design is inspired by Japanese paper-folding traditions—and the hexagonal seal and tag resemble Japanese heraldic crests. The use of authentic Japanese washi paper for the patterned triangle carries through the theme. If you don't have any washi paper handy, then substitute patterned origami paper or a suitable piece of gift wrap.

### 1. TRACE AND CUT OUT THE PATTERN
------------------------------------

Enlarge the bag pattern (see page 57) on a
photocopier, then trace it onto the back side of
a piece of pearlescent paper. At the same time,
enlarge the pattern for the gift tag and seal. Cut
out the bag. Mark fold lines in pencil. Also, cut
out a triangle from the patterned paper.

### 2. CREASE THE FOLDS; GLUE THE TRIANGLE
------------------------------------------

Using a ruler, crease all the fold lines. Next,
glue the decorative triangle onto the bag front,
the side with the flaps using a dry glue stick.

### 3. DRAW THE GOLD LINES
--------------------------

With the gold marker, outline the diagonal edge
of the triangle and the top edge of the bag. Use
a ruler to ensure straight lines, wiping it clean
with a towel after each marker line. Work over
a piece of scrap paper.

### 4. ASSEMBLE THE BAG
-----------------------

Turn the paper face down (white side up). Next,
fold the long flap down and apply glue stick
along its length (on the pearly side). Glue the
flap in place, folding it inside the bag.

## TIP

Use a cork-backed ruler to prevent the
marker ink from running under the ruler
and smudging. Or, stick several stacked
pieces of masking tape onto the back of
your ruler.

## 5. GLUE THE BOTTOM OF THE BAG

Glue the white side of the bottom bag flap (the shorter, wider flap). Fold it onto the bag back.

## 6. MAKE THE TAG AND BAG SEAL

Start with two plain white self-adhesive mailing labels. Use a dry glue stick to glue red pearlescent paper onto one label and matte gold paper onto the other. From each label, cut out a hexagon (use the pattern provided) and punch out a flower. Punch flower centers using the $1/4$" (6 mm) hand punch. To assemble each medallion, peel off the backing from the flower, then stick the flower onto a contrasting-colored hexagon. For the tag, cut out a slightly larger hexagon from yellow card stock. To complete the tag, peel off the backing from the flower medallion and center it on the tag. The remaining flower hexagon sticker is the bag seal; set it aside.

## 7. ATTACH THE TAG TO THE BAG

Using the $1/16$" (2mm) punch, make a hole at the upper right-hand corner of the bag, and another one at a tag corner. Cut 10" (25cm) of thin gold cord. Thread the cord through the tag hole, then tie the tag onto the bag. Trim the cord ends even. Seal the cord ends with a bit of crafter's glue if necessary.

## 8. FILL AND SEAL THE BAG

Insert the gift in the bag. (A flattish present is recommended!) Fold the bag top down on an angle as shown. Seal the bag with the hexagon flower sticker.

## Hex Marks the Spot

The hexagons for our bag seal and tag were cut using a craft knife and ruler following the pattern provided. However, if you are a scrapbooker, then you may already own the Coluzzle Cutting System and have a template for making hexagons in graduated sizes. If you prefer, use this method to cut geometrically perfect hexagons for the tag and seal.

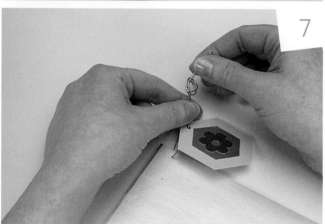

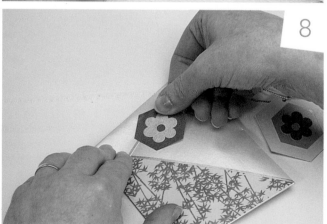

Enlarge the pattern 180%

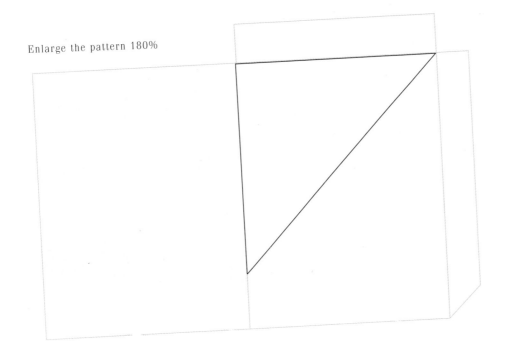

This pattern appears at full size.

## ✿ VARIATION IDEAS

Choose different paper patterns for a completely different look. Increase the size of the pattern for larger gifts.

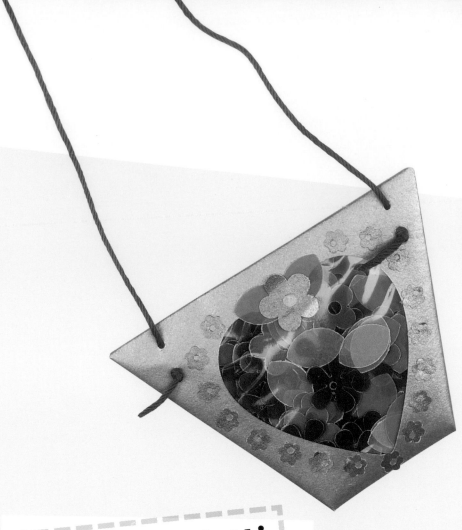

## MATERIALS LIST

### PAPER

Pearlescent paper in
pink and blue

Vellum in light and medium
green, pink and magenta

Cardstock (for template)

### ADDITIONAL SUPPLIES

Clear cellophane (sold by the
roll as gift wrap)

Matte embroidery cotton in blue

Self-adhesive mailing labels

Crafter's glue

Dry glue stick

Toothpicks

Shape cutter

Shape template: hearts

Craft knife

Self-healing cutting mat

Hand punches: 1/16" (2mm)
and 1/8" (3mm) circle;
1/4" (6mm) flower

Paper punches: assorted
flowers and leaf shapes

Metal ruler

Tapestry needle

# wedding confetti pouches

**D**istribute these dainty purse-style confetti pouches to wedding guests—and add an extra sprinkling of romance and fantasy to the special occasion! Made of shimmery pearlescent paper in delectable sugared-almond colors, each envelope-style pouch is decorated with a garland of punched paper posies surrounding a heart-shaped "picture window." Inside are delicate floral confetti shapes made of vellum.

Each confetti pouch starts off as a square of paper. Add a heart-shaped cutout, glue on the decorations, then make a few basic origami folds to produce the finished project.

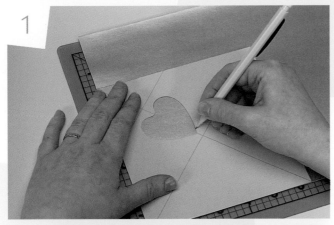

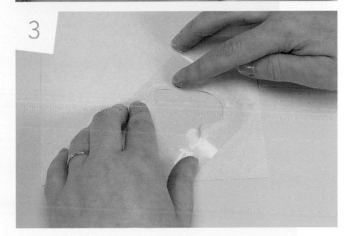

### 1. TRACE THE POUCH PATTERN ONTO PAPER
--------------------------------------------

Enlarge the confetti pouch pattern, given on page 63. Cut the heart-shaped cutout in the template using the shape cutter tool. Next, trace the pattern outline—including the heart shape—onto the pearly side of the pink paper.

### 2. CUT OUT THE HEART
----------------------

Cut the pouch square out of the pearly paper with your craft knife. Then cut out the heart using the 2" (5cm) heart-shaped template. For detailed shape cutter how-tos, see page 19.

### 3. GLUE CELLOPHANE BEHIND THE WINDOW
--------------------------------------------

Cut a small piece of cellophane to fit behind the heart window. On the back side of the paper, apply crafter's glue around the edges of the heart-shaped window. Center the cellophane over the window; smooth it in place carefully. Turn the paper over to check if any glue has crept onto the cellophane. Remove glue quickly with the tip of a toothpick or a moist piece of tissue.

**TIP**

*If you do not own a ShapeCutter tool, you can use an ordinary craft knife to cut out the heart shape.*

### 4. FOLD THE PAPER IN HALF

With the white side of the paper inside, fold the paper in half diagonally, forming a triangle. Crease the fold with your fingernail for a nice, crisp edge.

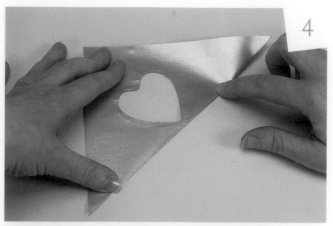

### 5. PUNCH OUT THE DECORATIVE FLOWERS

Begin by punching the flower centers, using the 1/16" (2mm) circle punch. Next, punch out the flower itself, centering the flower punch over the previously punched hole. Punch out seventeen flowers with the hand punch.

### 6. PUNCH THE SHAPES FOR THE CENTER FLOWER

Using the 1/8" (3mm) circle punch, punch one flower center in pink. Also punch out a five-petal flower from blue paper, and two leaf shapes from green vellum.

### 7. GLUE THE FLOWERS ONTO THE POUCH

Assemble the larger flower at the heart top in layers. Start with the larger flower at the heart top. Using crafter's glue, glue on two vellum leaves, followed by the five-petal flower. Next, glue on the pink flower center. Glue a small blue flower just below the bottom point of the heart window.

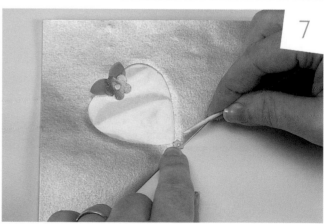

## TIP
*Turn the hand punch upside down and open the confetti catcher. You can now see if the hole is in the flower center.*

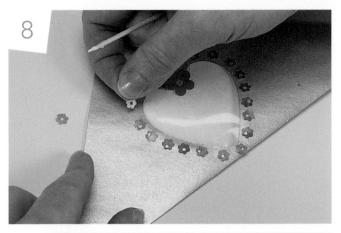

### 8. GLUE FLOWER GARLAND AROUND THE HEART
------------------------------------------------

After you have glued on the bottom flower, glue the remaining small flowers around the heart-shaped window, spacing them evenly apart.

### 9. FOLD THE POUCH
--------------------

With the window side face down, fold the right-hand triangle point across to meet the opposite side so the top and bottom edges of the paper are parallel. Crease the fold. Fold the left-hand triangle point over in a similar way, then crease the fold. Use a toothpick to glue beneath each triangle point and smooth the points down.

### 10. FOLD THE TOP FLAP
----------------------

On the back side of the pouch, fold the top corner down to form the envelope flap. Crease the fold.

## Posh Gift Packaging

*With just one small change, the pouch design can be adapted to make elegant gift packaging for a small item of jewelry—such as a ring, earrings or a delicate chain. Simply eliminate the window cutout to add the gift-giving "surprise factor." Replace the window with a glued-on heart-shaped cutout of the same size. Use pearlescent paper in a contrasting color.*

### 11. MARK HOLES FOR THE THREAD HANDLE
-------------------------------------------

At each corner of the pouch front, mark two holes spaced vertically, ¼" (6mm) apart. Open out the pouch top flap and punch the holes using the ¹⁄₁₆" (2mm) circle punch.

### 12. THREAD THE HANDLE
------------------------

Cut 18" (46cm) of matte embroidery cotton. Using a tapestry needle, thread each end of the handle through the holes. Knot the thread ends below the holes.

### 13. FILL THE POUCH WITH CONFETTI
---------------------------------------

Using a variety of flower and leaf shapes, punch out the confetti from the vellum. Alternatively, if you are really pushed for time, you can use purchased confetti. Fill the pouch with confetti. Make sure the confetti shows nicely through the window.

### 14. MAKE A FLOWER-SHAPED SEAL
------------------------------------

Glue a piece of blue pearly paper onto an adhesive label using a dry glue stick. Punch out a five-petal flower shape from the label. To complete the flower-shaped sticker, glue on a pink flower center using a ⅛" (3mm) circle. Seal down the back flap with the sticker.

## TIP
You can use six-strand embroidery floss as an alternative to matte embroidery cotton. Use all six strands.

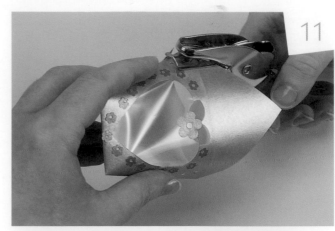

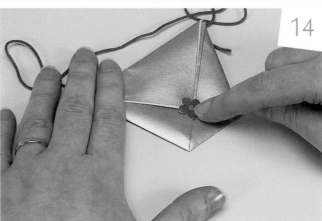

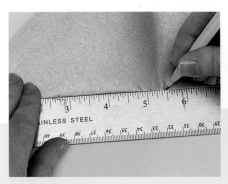  

**1. BEGIN THE FOLD**
- - - - - - - - - - - - - - - -

Once you've cut out the pattern and the heart shape, fold the pattern in half so it resembles a triangle. Mark the bottom edge of the triangle with dots, dividing it into thirds.

**2. MAKE THE SQUARE**
- - - - - - - - - - - - - - - -

Fold the right-hand point to meet the dot at left, aligning the bottom edges of the paper; crease the fold. Similarly, fold the left-hand point to meet the dot at right and crease the fold.

**3. CLOSE THE FLAP**
- - - - - - - - - - - - - - - -

Fold down the top flap. Reverse the color scheme of the square pouch so it complements the colors of the cup-shaped pouch.

❀ VARIATION: SQUARE CONFETTI POUCH
- - - - - - - - - - - - - - - - - - - - - - - - - - - - - - -

You can make a square pouch from the same pattern as the cup shape, simply by folding the triangle in a different way. Magic!

Enlarge the
pattern 200%.
You can use
it for both
the confetti
pouch and
the variation.

# sashiko cd gift box

Everybody enjoys receiving a CD, but a CD gift is a bit like getting a wrapped bottle of wine—no surprise—because of its easily recognizable shape and size. This attractive, reusable gift container brings back the surprise. It holds both a CD and its plastic case. It will show the recipient that you have spent as much thought and effort on packaging the gift as you did on selecting it.

This distinctive CD gift box is inspired by the boldly beautiful needle art of Japanese Sashiko quilting, in which designs are stitched onto contrasting-colored background fabric using large running stitches. For our box, we have chosen the traditional combination of white "stitching" on indigo. The hexagonal decorative medallions on the box are styled after Japanese heraldic crests.

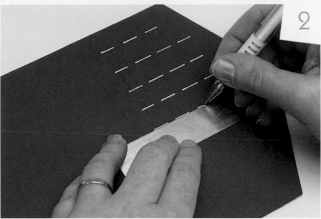

### 1. TRACE AND CUT OUT THE TEMPLATES
-------------------------------------

Enlarge the pattern templates on page 69 and make separate tracings for the two box pieces and the decorative hexagons. Trace and cut out the two box pieces from navy cardstock. Lightly score the fold lines as marked. Lay the tracings over the box pieces. Tape them in place with masking tape and with a stylus impress the "stitching lines". Use vertical dashes on the top flap, and horizontal dashes on the box bottom piece.

### 2. DRAW THE "STITCHING LINES"
-------------------------------

Use a white gel pen and a straightedge to draw the lines on the CD box pieces using the pattern you impressed in the previous step.

### 3. CREATE THE DECORATIVE CRESTS
---------------------------------

Trace and cut out the two larger hexagons from red paper and two smaller hexagons from white paper. Use the heart punch to make eight navy blue hearts. Punch out two ¼" (6mm) circles in red for the crest centers. With a dry glue stick, glue a white hexagon onto each red hexagon. Next, glue four blue hearts onto each white base. Glue a red dot in the center of each crest.

### 4. EMBELLISH THE BOX
--------------------

Use the pattern tracing to cut out the V-shaped box trim from the printed origami paper. Glue the origami trim onto the cover flap of the box using a dry glue stick. Trim the ends of the origami paper with scissors if necessary. Use crafter's glue to attach one decorative crest onto each box piece.

## TIP

*I used a craft knife and straightedge to cut out our hexagons, but you may wish to use nested templates, such as the Coluzzle Cutting System, to cut geometrically perfect hexagons.*

### 5. PUNCH A HOLE FOR THE TASSEL
--------------------------------

Use the ⅛" (3mm) punch to make a hole at the center of the box flap.

### 6. ASSEMBLE THE BOX
--------------------

Fold the box pieces along the scored lines, creasing firmly. Next, join the two box pieces. Apply crafter's glue to the underside of the bottom flap of the piece with horizontal dashes. Glue this onto the top flap of the piece that ends in the V-flap. Let the glue dry.

### 7. GLUE THE BOX SIDES
---------------------

One side at a time, apply glue to the outside of each flap, with the angled edge at the bottom. Fold up the box front and press each glued side flap onto the inside of the box back. Reach inside the box to smooth down the glued flaps. Use a rubber band to hold the box together until the glue sets.

## Prints Charming

*If you can't track down patterned origami paper for the box trim, substitute a scrapbooking print. You should be able to find a good selection of Asian-style motifs. (For example, check out Paper Adventures Quadrants Papercrafting Packs.) Or, use a suitable gift wrap pattern.*

### 8. CUT OUT THE TASSELS

On the back of a piece of red origami paper, measure a rectangle 2½" (6cm) wide by 4½" (11cm) long. Draw a ⅝" (16mm) border along the top of the rectangle. Cut along the bottom edge of the rectangle with scalloped paper edgers. Cut out the rest of the rectangle with a craft knife.

### 9. MARK THE TASSEL FRINGE

Draw a vertical line from each scallop indentation to the border, then draw another line from the lowest point of each scallop to the border.

### 10. CUT THE TASSEL FRINGE

Use small scissors to cut the fringe along the lines marked in the previous step.

### 11. ROLL THE TASSEL

Tightly roll the uncut top border of the tassel rectangle around a toothpick. When finished, secure the end with a dab of crafter's glue.

## Making Tassels

Tassels are easy to make and are a fantastic accent piece or embellishment for many paper-craft projects. Steps 8–13 can be used to make tassels for many of the projects in this book.

### 12. SECURE THE TASSEL

Cut a band of blue origami paper $1/8$" (3mm) wide by $1\frac{1}{2}$" (4cm) long. Wrap the band around the tassel top, just above the fringe. Glue the beginning and end of the band.

### 13. PUNCH A HOLE IN THE TASSEL

Flatten the tassel top, then punch a hole in the end of the tassel with a $1/16$" (2mm) punch. Make another tassel following steps 8–13.

### 14. TIE THE TASSELS ONTO THE BOX

Cut a 12" (30cm) piece of white embroidery cotton for each tassel. Fold the thread in half and thread the loop through a tapestry needle. Sew the loop through the tassel hole, then remove the needle and pull the thread ends through the loop. Repeat for the other tassel. Thread each tassel through the hole in the box flap. Knot the tassel threads on the back of the box and seal the knot with crafter's glue. To make a reclosable box seal, add a 3-D découpage self-adhesive foam pad under the point of the box flap.

## No-Hassle Tassels

The paper tassels on the box are fun and easy to make—but, if you prefer, inexpensive ready-made tassels made of silky thread are available at notions counters or in the home furnishings department. Or, make your own tassel substitute: Tie on a bit of rattail cord, and thread the ends with beads. Knot the rattail below the beads. Looks great!

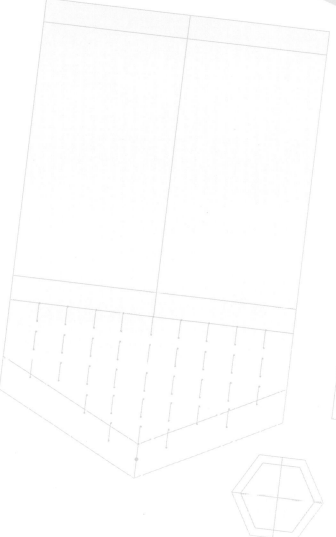

Enlarge the patterns 200%.

## ✿ VARIATION IDEA: BOX PAIR

To make a coordinating pair of CD gift boxes, use the templates for the red Sashiko CD box given on page 73. Its stitching lines go in opposite direction to those on the blue box.

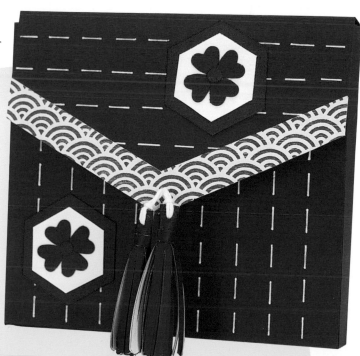

**PAPER**

One 12" × 12" (30cm × 30cm) sheet of red scrapbooking cardstock, or two 8½" × 11" (22cm × 28cm) sheets of scrapbooking cardstock

One sheet each of yellow and green paper

One sheet of mirrored cardstock

One square of red origami paper

**ADDITIONAL SUPPLIES**

Soft embroidery cotton in green

3-D découpage self-adhesive foam pad

Dry glue stick

Crafter's glue

Red and metallic green gel pens

Pencil

Toothpicks

Tapestry needle

Craft knife

Self-healing cutting mat

Paper edgers: scallop, clouds

Metal ruler

Paper punch: ½" (13mm) circle

Hand punches: ¹⁄₁₆" (2mm) and ⅛" (3mm) circles

Small scissors

# shisha cd gift box

Here is another take on the CD gift box (see page 64), this time finding its inspiration in the colorful mirror embroidery of India and Pakistan (see Shisha spangles, page 46). The tassel-trimmed gift box resembles a typical shisha-work purse (shisha means mirror).

The origin of mirror embroidery can be traced back to the folk belief that the mirrors were good-luck charms that warded off evil spirits. It was thought that the evil spirits were frightened off by seeing their own reflections!

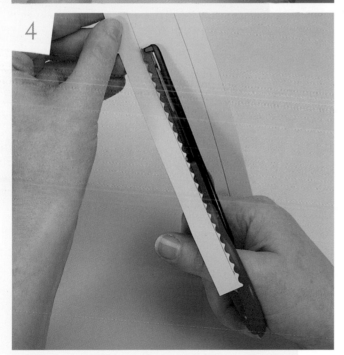

### 1. TRACE AND CUT OUT THE TEMPLATES

Enlarge the pattern templates on page 73 and make separate tracings for each of the two box pieces. Do not copy the dashes. They are for the Red Sashiko CD box variation. Trace and cut out the two box pieces from red cardstock. Lightly score the fold lines, then cut out the V-shaped flap using small-scallop paper edgers.

### 2. MAKE THE MOCK RICKRACK

Mark a straight line about 8" (20cm) long on a piece of green paper. Cut along the line with the clouds pattern (large scallops) paper edgers.

### 3. COMPLETE THE GREEN RICKRACK

To finish the rickrack band, cut another row of large scallops ¼" (6mm) below the first row. Position the paper edger blades so the scallop peaks are aligned with those in the first row. Make two more rickrack bands in this way.

### 4. CUT THE YELLOW BAND

On yellow paper, mark a band 1" (25mm) wide by about 8" (20cm) long. Cut the band out using the smaller scallop paper edgers. Make a second band in this way.

## What's Inside?

*Just because this box is CD-size doesn't mean you have to use it for its intended purpose. This box is the perfect size for small items of jewelry, such as bracelets or earrings. Or, it can be used as a container for small candy party favors.*

### 5. EMBELLISH THE BOX

Use a dry glue stick to glue the embellishments onto the box pieces. You will have to cut the flap bands to follow the edges of the box. Begin with the green decorative trim.

### 6. CONTINUE THE EMBELLISHMENT

Next, glue on the yellow decorative trim. For the perfect-fit miter join, cut one band to fit from V-point to edge with a diagonal cut.

### 7. FINISH THE DECORATIVE TRIM

Turn the cut side of the yellow strip over and join it at the V-point. Also glue a yellow band with rickrack to either side of the bottom of the box front.

### 8. ADD THE MIRRORED CIRCLES

Using the ½" (13mm) circle paper punch, punch out ten circles from mirrored cardstock. Use crafter's glue to attach the "mirrors" to the yellow bands. When gluing on a row of circles, glue the center circle first, then work your way outward to keep the spacing even.

## Perfect Cut!

*Steps 6–7 offer a simple way to make perfect miter-joined paper borders. You can use this to embellish anything from cards to scrapbook pages.*

## 9. DRAW THE GREEN DIAMONDS
--------------------------------

Use a green gel pen to draw double diamonds in between the mirror circles. First, draw an X in pencil, then complete the ends to make two adjacent diamonds. Color the diamonds in. Use a red gel pen to outline the mirror circles and draw "blanket stitch" spokes. To complete the CD box, follow steps 5–14 of the Sashiko CD Gift Box on page 66. Make the tassels in colors to match the box.

Enlarge the pattern 200%.

## ★ MATERIALS LIST

### PAPER

Gold embossed cardstock

Red cardstock

Scrapbooking paper: a Christmas print

Small amount of green vellum (for holly leaf)

Small amount of dark green elephant hide (for leaf)

### ADDITIONAL SUPPLIES

3-D découpage self-adhesive foam pads

22" (56cm) of green velvety cord

Five 1/4" (6mm) diameter round red beads

One small gold jingle bell

8" (20cm) of 1/8" (3mm) wide metallic gold taffeta ribbon

Dry glue stick

Crafter's glue

Toothpicks

Metallic gold marker (fine point)

Pencil

Kneaded eraser

Tapestry needle

Sewing needle and thread (for sewing on bow)

Shape cutter

Self-healing cutting mat

Shape template: stars

Paper crimper

Craft knife

Paper edger: scallop pattern

Hand punch: 1/16" (2mm) circle

# starburst ornament

**W**ith the help of a shape cutter tool, you can quickly craft a tree full of these cheery three-dimensional "starburst" ornaments. Or if you prefer, hang them in doorways or in the window where the breeze will set the loop-top jingle bell tinkling.

Fans of 3-D découpage will find this project to be a special treat. Each ornament is comprised of a triple-decker arrangement of star cut outs in coordinating festive papers.

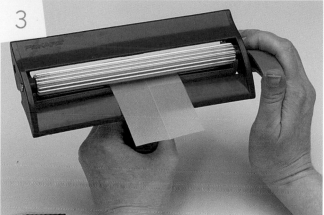

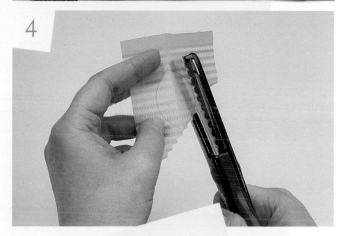

### 1. CUT OUT THE STARS

Using the shape cutter, cut out three stars: one 3" (8cm), one 4" (10cm) and one 4½" (11cm). Use the gold embossed cardstock for the largest star and red cardstock for the medium star. For the smallest star, bond printed scrapbooking paper onto the red cardstock using a dry glue stick.

### 2. ATTACH THE STARS

Using the fine-point metallic gold marker, outline the two smaller stars. Then use the 3-D découpage self-adhesive foam pads to connect the stars. The largest (gold embossed) star is the bottom. Place a pad on the underside of each arm of the medium-size red star, but set it back a bit so the pad is not visible. Stick the red star onto the gold star, turning it slightly off center. Stick the smallest star on top, twisting it the same way.

### 3. CRINKLE PAPER FOR THE LEAVES

Cut out small rectangles of green vellum and dark green elephant hide (or, use flocked paper as an alternative). Crease the paper rectangles in half vertically. Feed each rectangle through the paper crimper with the crease in the vertical position. (For further instructions on how to use a paper crimper, see page 21.)

### 4. CUT OUT THE LEAVES

Cut out a leaf template (see page 77) from cardstock. Trace a leaf outline onto each piece of crinkled paper. Make sure you align the paper fold with the points of the leaf shape. Use scalloped paper edgers to cut out each leaf. Since these are holly leaves, you need to make concave scallops to create the pointy edges. To do this, hold the paper edger upside down to cut. Once done, use a kneaded eraser to gently remove the pencil marks.

## Sticky Pad Alternative

*An economical alternative to using foam sticky pads is to make your own spacers by cutting little snippets of cardboard from a cardboard box. Attach these with crafter's glue.*

### 5. GLUE THE LEAVES TOGETHER

Glue the dark green holly leaf on top of the vellum leaf, matching leaf points at one end as shown.

### 6. MAKE HOLES IN THE LEAF

Using a ¹⁄₁₆" (2mm) hand punch, make two holes in the center of the darker leaf, ³⁄₄" (19mm) apart. Position the holes on the paper fold. Take 12" (30cm) of green velvet cord and lace it through the holes with the cord ends on top of the leaves. If you wish, thread the cord through a tapestry needle for easier lacing. Green yarn can be substituted for the velvet cord as an easy-to-find alternative.

### 7. ADD THE BEADS

Thread three red beads onto the cord nearest the overlapping leaf points. Slide the beads down the cord to the point where the cord emerges from the leaf. Knot the cord just below the beads.

### 8. ADD BEADS TO THE CORD ENDS

Thread a bead onto each of the cord ends. Knot each cord below the bead. Trim off any extra cord, then glue the leaves onto the center of the top star using crafter's glue.

## Star Alternative

*If you don't own a shape cutter tool, another way to cut stars in stepped sizes is to use a graduated-size template and knife set, such as the Coluzzle Cutting System. Using this method, you hand-cut the stars using a craft knife.*

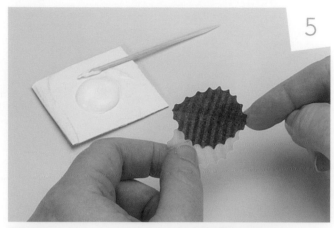

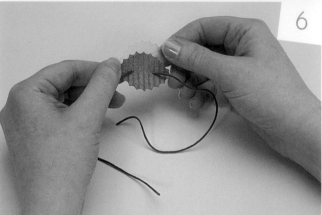

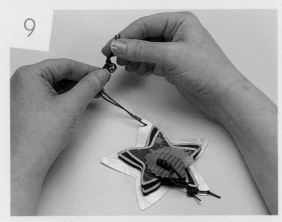

## 9. ADD THE HANGING LOOP

Punch a ¹⁄₁₆" (2mm) hole for the hanging cord at the top of the bottom (gold embossed) star. Thread 10" (25cm) of green cord through the hole. Next, add the jingle bell. Thread both cord ends through the loop on the jingle bell. Knot the cord so the jingle bell is contained by the knot.

## 10. ADD A BOW

Make a bow with 8" (20cm) of ¹⁄₈" (3mm) wide gold taffeta ribbon. Sew this through the cord knot just below the jingle bell.

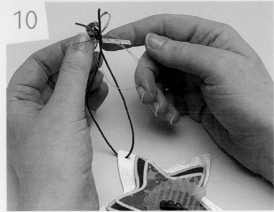

### Starry Garland

For a party decoration, make a garland by stringing a group of star-shaped ornaments side by side. Simply punch holes in opposite star points and tie the stars together. If you prefer, string the stars vertically and hang the cascade from the ceiling. A cascade is particularly effective with stars in graduated sizes.

## ✿ VARIATION IDEA: STARRY CELEBRATIONS

Make the star ornament in non-Christmas colors to suit other occasions such as birthdays, anniversaries, job promotions or graduations. Instead of going for gold, try a silver color scheme. Track down scrapbooking paper in an event-specific print. In place of holly leaves, glue a charm onto the center of the top star (add a mini bow to conceal the loop at the top of the charm). You can also use the star ornament to dress up a gift box, or as a detachable ornament on the cover of a homemade greeting card.

This pattern appears at full size.

## ⭐ MATERIALS LIST

### PAPER

Gold embossed gift wrap

Scrapbooking paper:
a Christmas print

Small amount of green vellum
(for holly leaf)

Small amount of dark green
elephant hide (for leaf)

### ADDITIONAL SUPPLIES

30" (76cm) of velvety cord
in green

Five ¼" (6mm) diameter
round red beads

8" (20cm) of ⅛" (3mm)
wide metallic gold taffeta ribbon

Dry glue stick

Crafter's glue

Metallic gold marker
(fine point)

Stapler

Tapestry needle

Sewing needle and thread
(for sewing on bow)

Shape cutter

Self-healing cutting mat

Shape template: stars

Metal ruler

Hand punch: ¹⁄₁₆" (2mm)
and ⅛" (3mm) circle

Paper crimper

Paper edgers: scallop

# stars foldout ornament

Here's another easy Christmas ornament craft-ed from ShapeCutter stars. Since this orna-ment can be viewed from all sides, it is ideal for hanging in a doorway, like mistletoe.

This ornament also looks great in holographic card-stock backed with velvety flocked paper. The latest velvety papers are very realistic-looking—they have a classy suede finish—and come in a good range of col-ors. Check some out next time you are in a scrapbook-ing store.

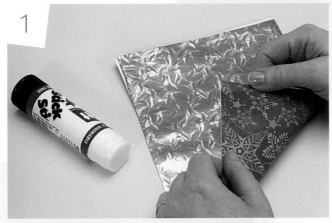

### 1. PREPARE THE PAPER

Glue a piece of gold embossed gift wrap and a piece of Christmas-print scrapbook paper together back-to-back, so it becomes double-sided. If you wish, you can use gold cardstock instead of gift wrap.

### 2. CUT OUT THE STARS

Use the shape cutter to cut out four 4" (10cm) stars and two 1½" (38mm) stars using the double-sided paper you created in step 1. Use the metallic gold marker to out-line the Christmas-print side of the stars.

### 3. FOLD THE STARS

Fold the four larger stars in half. Since the double-sided paper is fairly lightweight there is no need to score the folds. (If, however, you use gold cardstock, you will need to score the folds.) Use a straightedge to keep the folds neat and crisp.

### 4. STAPLE THE STARS TOGETHER

Lay the four large stars on top of each other with points and folds aligned. Lay the first two stars with the gold side face up, and the last two stars with the print side face up. Once done, staple the stars together along the center fold; place one staple near the top and the other near the bottom.

### 5. ADD THE CORD

Punch two holes with the $\frac{1}{8}$" (3mm) hole punch through all the stars, one near the top, and another at the bottom. Cut 12" (30cm) of green velvet cord. Fold the cord in half and pass the loop end through the hole. Next, pass the cord ends through the loop and pull them tight to secure them. Pull the cords gently so you don't damage the star.

### 6. ATTACH THE SMALL STARS

Using the $\frac{1}{16}$" (2mm) hole punch, punch two holes in each of the two small stars. Punch one hole in a star point and the second hole about $\frac{1}{4}$" (6mm) below the first. Pass a cord through the holes in a star, thread on a bead, then knot the cord just below the bead. Attach a second star to the remaining cord end in the same way, but tie it on at a different length for variety. Trim the cord ends.

### 7. MAKE THE LEAVES

Create two holly leaves as for the Starburst Ornament on page 75, steps 3 and 4. Use the 1/16" (2mm) hand punch to make one hole near the bottom of the vellum leaf and two holes, spaced equally apart, on the center fold of the darker leaf.

### 8. THREAD THE LEAVES

Cut 18" (46cm) of green velvet cord, then thread the cord through the hole in the star point. Make sure the cord ends are level, then thread the cord through the bottom hole of both leaves, placing the darker leaf on top of the vellum leaf. Thread three beads onto the cord and slide them down to where the cord emerges from the hole in the darker leaf.

### 9. PULL THE CORD THROUGH

Draw the cord with the beads through the remaining hole on the dark leaf and then back through the single hole on the vellum leaf. Pull the cord so the beads are held snugly against the leaf.

### 10. ADD THE BOW

Knot both cords together, just above the leaves and tie another knot near the ends of the cord. This forms a hanging loop. Create a bow from 8" (20cm) of 1/8" (3mm) wide gold taffeta ribbon. Sew it onto the knot at the top of the hanging loop. Open out the folds of the star before hanging the ornament, for maximum three-dimensional effect.

## Great Shapes

*Foldout ornaments can be made in different shapes for use on holidays and special occasions. Simply choose a different shape template. For example, use hearts for Valentine's Day, or make gift-box-shaped ornaments out of rectangles for use as birthday decorations.*

You can use this technique to make so much more than just ornaments. These two cards were made using a diamond shape template to make the hole in the card. The diamond template was also used to make the three-dimensional ornaments in the middle using the same techniques as the Star Foldout Ornament. As embellishments, I added a bow and bead at the top of the diamond. If you use archival quality paper, these cards are sure to become keepsakes!

## ✿ VARIATION IDEA: TREE ORNAMENT

The two-tone effect of this Christmas tree ornament is really eye-catching. Plus, the visual pun of hanging a mini tree on a real Christmas tree is smile-worthy. The tree template can be found on the Fiskars Christmas shape template. You will need green cardstock and red velvet cord for this project.

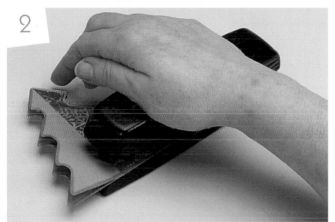

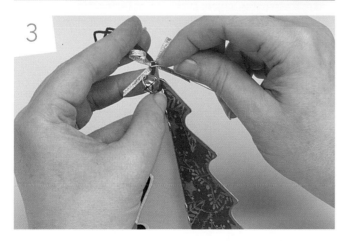

### 1. CUT OUT THE TREE

First, prepare the two-toned paper. Glue a piece of red scrapbooking print onto a piece of green scrapbooking cardstock so there is a straight line between them. Align the straight line with the center of the tree template. Cut out two trees this way. Outline the tree with metallic gold marker on both sides.

### 9. SCORE, FOLD AND STAPLE THE TREES

Score the tree shapes down the center where the papers join, then fold them in half. Next, place the trees back-to-back and staple them together. Place one staple near the top and another near the bottom, but not too close to the edge, so they will be less visible.

### 3. ADD THE HANGING LOOP

Punch a ⅛" (3mm) hole at the top of the tree. Cut 14" (36cm) of red velvet cord and pass it through the hole. Thread both ends through the loop on the jingle bell. Knot the cord so the jingle bell is contained by the knot. Make a mini bow from 8" (20cm) of ⅛" (3mm) wide gold taffeta ribbon and sew it onto the knot in the cord.

**PAPER**

Two 8½" × 11" (22cm × 28cm) sheets of red scrapbooking cardstock

Small pieces of scrapbooking paper in green and white prints. You need five different patterns.

One sheet of matte gold metallic paper

**ADDITIONAL SUPPLIES**

22" (50cm) of gold cord

12" (30cm) of ½" (13mm) wide gold taffeta ribbon

Crafter's glue

Dry glue stick

Pencil

Kneaded eraser

Toothpicks

Rubber band

Tapestry needle

Needle and thread

Craft knife

Self-healing cutting mat

Metal ruler

Hand punches: ¹⁄₁₆" (2mm) and ⅛" (3mm) circles

Circle cutter (compass-style)

Small scissors

Paper edgers: scallop

# cathedral window ornament

This cube-shaped holiday ornament has the look of cathedral window patchwork, a needlecraft technique prized for its intricate-looking, beautiful and dimensional appearance.

The wonderful selection of printed scrapbooking papers available makes paper patchwork projects like this one a pleasure to create. Here a mix of green-and-white checks and florals has been used, but you could just as easily opt for a seasonal selection of Christmas-motif papers. Have a browse around your local scrapbooking supplier—and explore the paper patchwork possibilities!

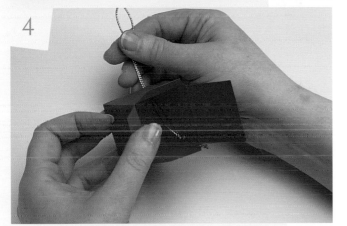

### 1. TRACE AND CUT OUT THE PATTERN

Enlarge and trace the cube pattern (given on page 89). Transfer the pattern outline and markings onto the red cardstock. Use a craft knife and ruler to cut out the pattern. Lightly score the fold lines.

### 2. PUNCH A HOLE

Use the ⅛" (3mm) hand punch to make a hole in the pattern (indicated by a dot). Next, use a kneaded eraser to remove any pencil lines from the cube pattern.

### 3. ASSEMBLE THE CUBE

Crease the scored folds of the box pattern, then assemble the cube. First, glue under the flap on the long strip to make a four-sided ring. Next, glue down one side of the cube, but leave the opposite side unglued. Use crafter's glue applied with a toothpick. Use a rubber band to hold the cube in place as the glue dries.

### 4. ADD THE HANGING LOOP

You must attach the hanging loop to the ornament before you close the cube. To do this, cut a 12" (30cm) piece of gold cord. Make a loop and knot the end three times, making a bulky knot. Starting from inside the cube, feed the loop carefully through the hole, making sure the knot remains inside. Once the loop is attached, fold down and glue the last side of the cube.

## TIP

*If you are going to make more than one ornament, it is advisable to make a trace-around template for the cube out of cardstock.*

### 5. CUT OUT THE CIRCLES

Using the circle cutter, carefully cut out six circles from red cardstock, each measuring $2\frac{1}{8}$" (52mm) diameter, a radius of $1\frac{1}{16}$" (26mm).

### 6. CUT OUT THE PRINTED SQUARES

Cut out six squares, $1\frac{1}{2}$" (38mm) on each side, from the decorative paper. You need five different printed patterns. Cut four squares from different prints and two squares from the same print. The squares fit perfectly in the circles. Glue a square onto each circle using a dry glue stick. Trim the squares, if necessary, to make sure they look neat.

### 7. SCORE AND FOLD THE CIRCLE EDGES

Lightly score the red cardstock along all four sides of each square. Next, crease along the scored lines, folding the edges of the circle in toward the center of the square. This completes the Cathedral Window patch.

## TIP

Five different prints may seem like a lot, but you can buy reversible scrapbooking paper with double-sided coordinating prints—so you can get two different prints from a single sheet of paper.

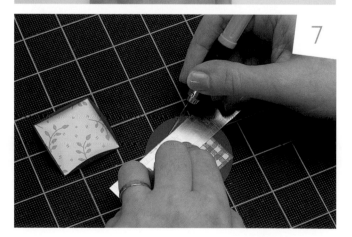

### 8. CUT A HOLE FOR THE TASSEL
--------------------------------

At the cube corner directly opposite the hanging loop, use scissors to cut a small hole. This is for the tassel cord.

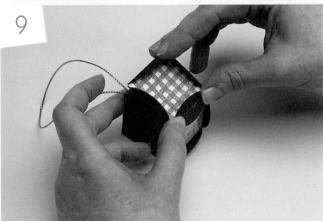

### 9. GLUE ON THE DECORATIVE SIDES
------------------------------------

Using crafter's glue applied with a toothpick, glue a Cathedral Window patch onto each side of the cube. Glue the two identical prints onto opposite sides of the cube.

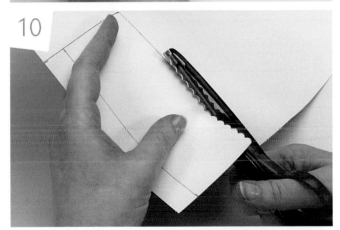

### 10. MAKE A TASSEL
----------------------

On the back of a piece of matte gold paper, measure a rectangle $2\frac{1}{2}$" (6cm) wide by $4\frac{1}{2}$" (11cm) long. Draw a $\frac{5}{8}$" (16mm) border along the top of the rectangle. Cut the bottom edge of the rectangle with scalloped paper edgers. Cut out the rest of the rectangle with a craft knife.

### 11. MARK THE TASSEL
------------------------

Draw a vertical line from each scallop indentation to the border, then draw another line from the lowest point of each scallop to the border.

### 12. CUT THE TASSEL FRINGE

Use small scissors to cut the fringe along the lines marked in the previous step.

### 13. ROLL THE TASSEL

Tightly roll the uncut top border of the tassel around a toothpick. When finished, secure the end with a dab of crafter's glue.

### 14. COMPLETE THE TASSEL

Cut a band of decorative print paper $\frac{1}{8}$" (3mm) wide by $1\frac{1}{2}$" (38mm) long. Wrap the band around the tassel top, just above the fringe. Glue the beginning and end of the band. Next, flatten the tassel top and punch a hole through it with the $\frac{1}{16}$" (2mm) hand punch.

### 15. ATTACH THE TASSEL

Cut a 10" (25cm) piece of gold cord and thread it through the tassel hole. Tie a few knots in the cord, just above the tassel. Once done, push the knot through the small hole you made at the corner of the cube and secure it with a bit of crafter's glue. For the finishing touch, cut a 12" (30cm) piece of $\frac{1}{2}$" (13mm) ribbon and tie a bow. Sew the bow onto the hanging loop at the top of the ornament.

**TIP**

The eye of a tapestry needle or the tip of small scissors can be used to push the knot through the hole.

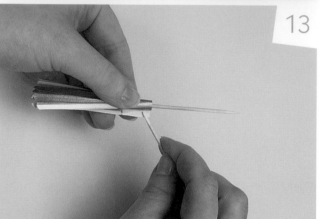

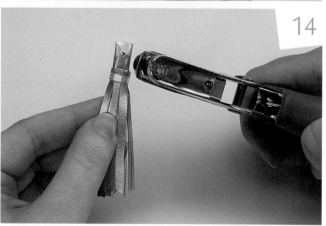

### ❀ VARIATION IDEA: QUICK-MAKE ORNAMENT

Glue a Cathedral Window patch onto a cardstock circle with a 1¹/₁₆" (26mm) radius, same size as for the patch backing. Punch holes at the top and bottom, then add a hanging loop and tassel. This ornament is compact, so it can easily fit inside an envelope. Send it as a greeting card enclosure.

### ❀ VARIATION IDEA: JUMBO ORNAMENT

Display this large-size ornament in a window or doorway. To make it, size up the cube pattern so that each face measures 3" (75mm). Glue on Cathedral Window patches four to a side (you will need a total of 24 patches). For the finishing touch, add a silky purchased tassel.

Enlarge the pattern 118%.

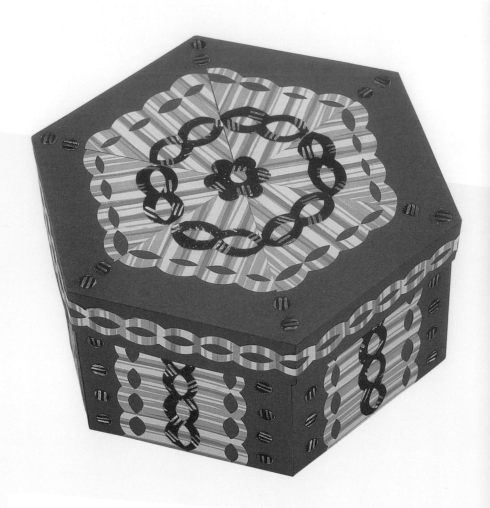

# paper chain gift box

I t's time to play the chain game. This elegant fili-gree-effect gift box is embellished with paper chains fashioned with paper edgers. They are sim-ilar to the paper snowflakes and the chorus lines of linked paper dolls you made as a child.

The pleasing hexagonal shape of this gift box gives the medallion on the lid a snowflake appearance. The designs on the side panels and the box lid are coordi-nated using two scrapbook prints.

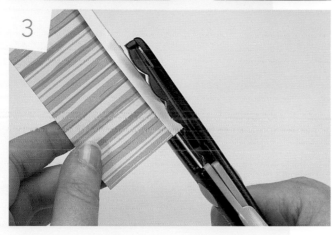

### 1. TRACE AND CUT OUT THE BOX AND LID
------------------------------------------

Enlarge the patterns on page 97 onto tracing paper. Tape each pattern piece onto a piece of forest green scrapbooking cardstock. Impress the pattern outlines and markings into the cardstock, using a stylus. Use a craft knife and ruler to cut out the box and lid. Then score the fold lines as marked.

### 2. CUT OUT THE DECORATIVE SIDE PANELS
------------------------------------------

On the back (the plain side) of the striped scrapbooking paper, measure out and mark in pencil six 2" × 3" (5cm × 8cm) rectangles. Make sure the stripes run perpendicular to the long dimension of the rectangle (see photo). On the long sides of the rectangle, make a pencil line margin $\frac{1}{4}$" (6mm) in from either edge. Cut out the rectangles using a craft knife and ruler.

### 3. CUT THE SIDE PANEL BORDER
------------------------------------------

Fold the side of the rectangle at the margin. Use the clouds (large scallop) paper edgers to cut along the fold. Do not cut to the full depth of the blade; cut with the tip of each scallop only. You must position the blade on the fold so the paper is cut just part of the way through. You must cut curved chunks out of the paper with little "bridges" in between. After each cut, reposition the blade for the next cut. Aim to cut to a consistent depth, so the cutouts are of uniform size. Cut both sides of the rectangle this way.

## TIP

*Making paper chains is more difficult to explain than to do! Do a few scrap-paper test runs and you'll soon master the technique.*

### 4. COMPLETE THE SIDE PANEL BORDERS

Unfold the sides of the paper and use the paper edgers to cut a scalloped edge. Make sure to align the paper edger blade to echo the shape of the previous cutouts. Repeat for the other side of the panel. Make five more side panels, following steps 2–4.

### 5. CUT THE PAPER CHAIN TRIM

From the green striped paper, cut two strips, each measuring 1" (25mm) wide by 12" (30cm) long (the full width of the scrapbooking paper). The stripes should run crosswise across each strip. Fold each strip in half lengthwise and cut along the fold using the clouds paper edgers. Use the partial-cutting technique described in step 3. Remember, if you cut to the full depth of the scallops, the two sides of the strip will fall apart! Cut two 12" (30cm) strips of the rust-colored paper in the same way.

### 6. EDGE THE STRIP

Open out the fold. To complete the paper chain, cut a scalloped edge to either side of the leaf-shaped cutouts. Align the scallops to echo the curves of the leaf shapes. Turn the strip around to edge the second side of the chain. You need to make two green chains and two rust-colored chains in order to complete the box decoration.

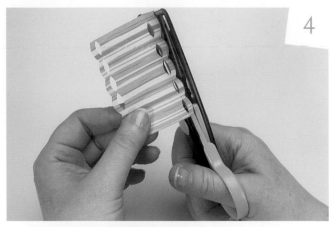

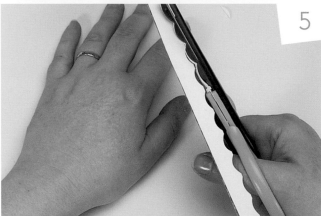

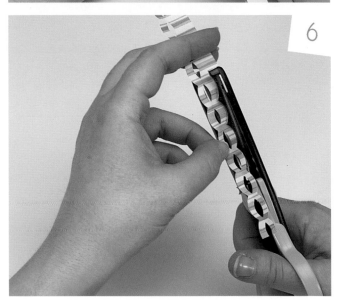

## Faking It

*The following method of cutting a paper chain is a bit of a cheat—but it looks great! First, cut out a narrow strip of paper and crease it in half lengthwise. Next, cut paper-edged borders on either side. Finally, fake a chain effect by using a hand punch to cut out regularly spaced decorative shapes down the center of the paper strip; use the crease as a positioning guide. You can use hearts, squares, stars—whatever motif suits the blade pattern!*

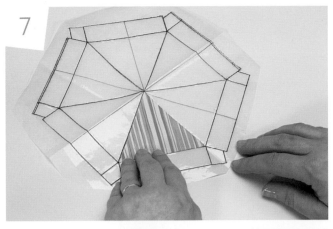

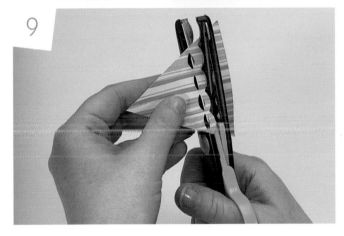

### 7. CUT OUT THE TRIANGLES

You need six paper triangles for the lid medallion. Cut them out from the striped green paper using the lid pattern. Position the stripes so they run vertically from the tip to the base of the triangle.

### 8. FOLD AND CUT THE TRIANGLES

On the back of a triangle, mark a ¾" (19mm) margin along the base. Fold the margin to the right side and cut it as for step 3.

### 9. EDGE THE TRIANGLE

Open out the triangle and cut scallops along the base, echoing the curves of the leaf-shaped cutouts.

## Chain Reaction

Experiment with different paper edger blades to create some extraordinary paper chain results! Results can vary from the plain and simple to dizzyingly complex-looking effects. Chains can be crafted in different styles and period looks. For example: Fiskars Lightning pattern blades make V-shaped chain links; the Victorian pattern makes ornate links; and the Peaks pattern has a distinctly Art Deco feel. More intricate designs call for greater care and may require extra pressure while cutting.

## 10. MARK AND CUT CHAINS ON THE OTHER TRIANGLES

Use the triangle you have just finished as a template. Trace the cutout border design onto the back of the five remaining triangles. Next, fold and cut the triangles as for steps 7–9, but align your cuts with the traced outlines. This ensures that the triangles will fit together perfectly when they are glued side by side on the box lid.

## 11. CUT THE RUST-COLORED CHAINS

To embellish the box, you must cut the paper chains into smaller link strips. For each triangle, cut two links of the rust chain. For each side panel, cut four rust links. Trim the ends of each link strip into a leaf-tip shape. There are six triangles and six side panels.

## 12. PUNCH OUT THE DECORATIVE CIRCLES

Use the 1/4" (6mm) hole punch to cut decorative circles for the box lid and sides from the rust-colored paper. You need a total of seventy-two rust-colored circles. Position the punch on the printed paper pattern so that a particular area of the design falls on the circle. You also need to punch out one green circle and a 1" (25mm) flower from the rust-colored paper.

**TIP**

If you accidentally smudge a bit of glue stick on the box, remove it with a kneaded eraser while the glue is fresh.

10

11

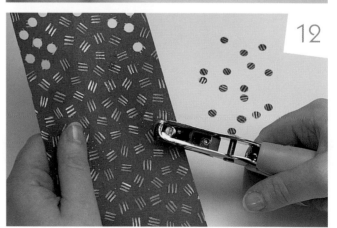

12

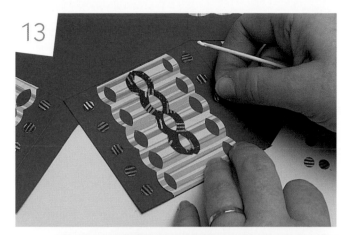

13

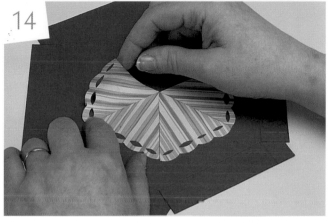

14

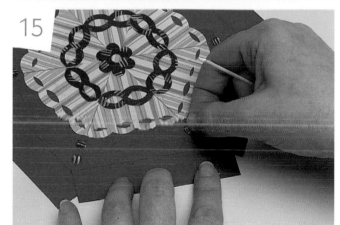

15

### 13. DECORATE THE BOX SIDES

Glue the side panels onto the base of the box using a dry glue stick. Center a panel on each side. In the center of each panel, glue on four rust-colored chain links, as shown. Finally, glue on the dots to the sides of each panel using crafter's glue applied with a toothpick.

### 14. GLUE ON THE TRIANGLES

Glue the triangles onto the lid with a dry glue stick. Glue the tip of each triangle at the center of the lid. Position the triangles side-by-side, like pizza wedges.

### 15. DECORATE THE LID

Use a dry glue stick to attach the lid decorations. Glue the flower on at the center, then glue the rust-colored links onto each triangle. Align the rust links horizontally so they meet up to form a continuous chain around the lid. Glue on the circles using crafter's glue. Glue on the green circle for the flower center.

### 16. FOLD THE LID

Crease the sides of the lid along the scored lines. Remember to fold the little tabs.

### 17. GLUE THE LID TOGETHER

Use crafter's glue, applied with a toothpick, to glue the lid together. Apply glue to the top of each little flap, then glue the flaps under. Use masking tape to hold the lid in place until the glue dries.

### 18. DECORATE THE SIDE OF THE LID

Apply the green paper chain to the side of the box lid using a dry glue stick. You will need both strips of green chain. The end links of the two strips can be glued side by side. Trim off any excess links.

### 19. ASSEMBLE THE BOX

Fold the box base along the scored lines. Glue the sides together using crafter's glue. Again, a piece of tape will hold the box together while the glue dries.

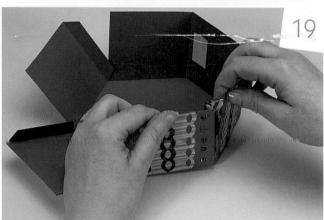

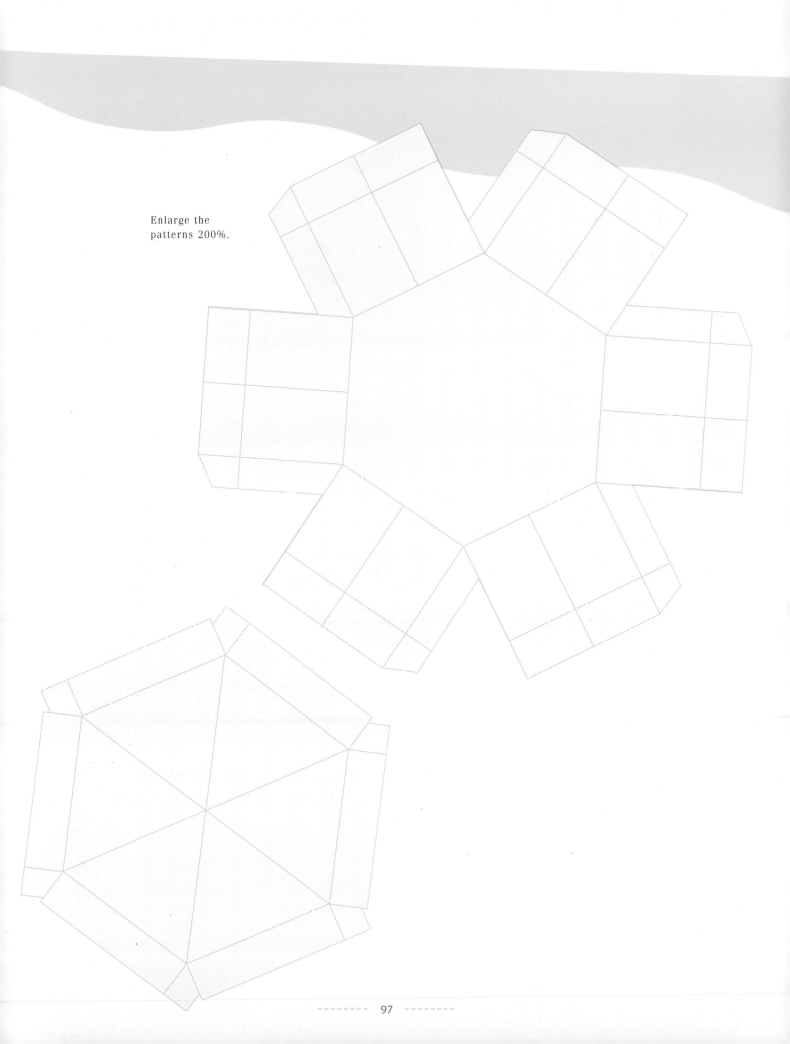

Enlarge the
patterns 200%.

**MATERIALS LIST**

**PAPER**

Matte silver pearlescent
cardstock

White pearlescent paper

White illustration board
or heavyweight cardboard

**ADDITIONAL SUPPLIES**

Self-adhesive white
mailing labels, 3" × 5"
(8cm × 13cm)

Dry glue stick

Crafter's glue

Pencil

Tracing paper

Masking tape

Stylus

Toothpicks

Metal ruler

Craft knife

Self-healing cutting mat

Shape cutter

Shape template: ovals

Corner edgers: celestial

Paper punches: $^1/_2$" (13mm)
and 1" (25mm) hearts

Small scissors

Hand punches: $^1/_4$" (6mm)
and $^1/_8$" (3mm) circles

# etched-glass photo frame

This pretty "etched-glass mirror" photo frame has the quaint, charming appearance of a bygone era. The frame makes a beautiful—mailable—gift presentation for a commemorative photograph and is perfect for special family occasions, such as anniversaries, birthdays or Mother's Day. Send it in place of a card: You can inscribe the frame back with your good wishes! Designed to fit a standard 4" × 6" (10cm × 15cm) snapshot, the frame can be used in either portrait or landscape direction.

For our frame, we chose matte-finish silvery pearlescent cardstock for a lustrous, quietly classy look—but you can go for glitz with highly reflective mirrored card!

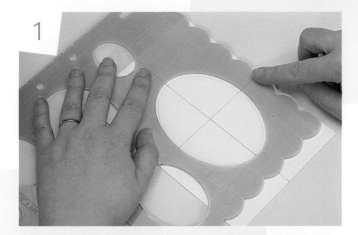

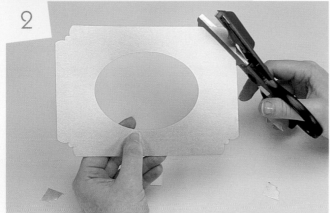

*The choice of frame cardstock is your call. You can opt for a high-gloss mirror effect or a subtle matte silver pearlescent look. For a classy total effect, have your photo finished—gloss or matte—to match the frame. Attention to detail makes a gift special.*

### 1. CUT OUT THE OVAL FRAME

Enlarge the frame pattern (see page 103) and make a pattern tracing (there are three pieces: the frame, the backing, and the strut). On the back of the silver cardstock (the white side), mark the 5" × 7" (13cm × 18cm) frame rectangle and the crisscross positioning lines. Cut out the frame rectangle using a craft knife held against a ruler. Position the frame behind the oval template. The size of the oval is 3" × 4" (8cm × 10cm), centering the criss-cross lines on the oval template. Cut out the oval using a shape cutter tool.

### 2. TRIM THE CORNERS

Use the corner edgers to cut the decorative corners of the frame. To do this, inspect the edgers and check that the blades are on the correct side to cut a convex (inward-facing) scallop. Next, open the edgers and slide the corner of the cardstock underneath the guide slot until the cardstock is flush with the edges of the guide. Cut the corner, then repeat for the remaining three corners.

### 3. BOND A PEARLESCENT STICKER

Use a dry glue stick to glue the white pearlescent paper to the self-adhesive mailing label. Glue the matte side of the pearlescent paper to the paper side of the sticker. Make three stickers in this way.

### 4. PUNCH OUT THE LARGE HEARTS

You need to make two outline heart stickers for the frame. To begin the outline heart, punch a ½" (13mm) heart out of the pearlescent sticker. Next, center a 1" (25mm) heart punch over the smaller heart-shaped cutout. Use the heart punch on the back so you can see how to position it. Punch out the heart. Repeat to make a second outline heart.

### 5. PUNCH OUT THE OTHER PEARLY STICKERS

In addition to the two outline hearts (above), you also need to punch two more 1" (25mm) hearts. Cut these in half vertically using small scissors. Also punch out sixteen small hearts and two ¼" (6mm) circles from the pearly stickers. Cut four of the small heart stickers in half.

### 6. TRACE THE DECORATIVE PATTERN

Tape your pattern tracing over the silver side of the frame using masking tape. Next, use a stylus to impress small dots to mark the position of each heart sticker. Make a dot at the point and the "valley" of each heart. Also mark the position of the pearly dots.

### 7. ADD THE HEART STICKERS

Peel off the backing from each heart sticker and, using the impressed dots as a guide, smooth the hearts onto the frame where indicated. Use the pattern tracing as a "map" to show the placement of each sticker (for example, which direction each heart faces). Also affix the two ¼" (6mm) circles.

## TIP

*No need to mark the heart outlines on the frame. The placement dots work just as well and are less likely to show when the stickers are covering them.*

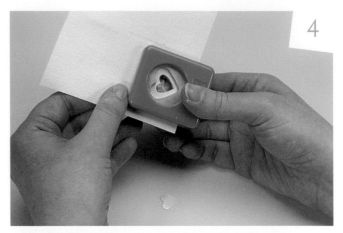

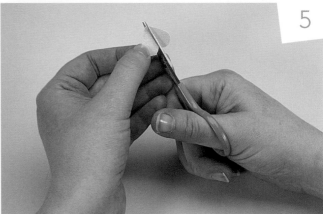

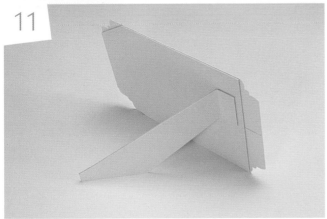

### 8. ADD THE SMALL CIRCLES

Use the $1/8$" (3mm) hand punch to cut out sixteen small circles from the pearlescent paper. Use crafter's glue to apply them to the frame at the marked dots. Use a toothpick to apply the glue sparingly. These circles are glued on because they are too small to make as stickers.

### 9. ADD THE BACKING

Using the pattern, trace and cut out the backing card and the strut from illustration board. The backing is the same size as the frame, with the corners trimmed so that the backing does not show beyond the frame. You may also need to trim the top for easy picture insertion. Glue the frame to the backing. Use a toothpick to sparingly apply crafter's glue around three of the straight sides of the backing. Leave one of the short sides unglued, as this is the picture opening.

### 10. GLUE ON THE STRUT

Score the strut tab, but not too deeply, as the strut must support the frame. Once done, use crafter's glue to apply the strut to the back of the frame. Glue the strut onto the backing. The bottom of the strut should just touch the edge of the frame, and the tab is glued just below the open edge of the backing, to the left of backing center. To finish, gently slip the photograph into the frame opening.

### 11. OPEN THE STRUT

To display the frame, just open the strut and place it on the table. You may have to make a few adjustments to the strut to get the angle of the picture correct. The frame can be displayed both horizontally and vertically.

##  VARIATION IDEA: THE FRAME GAME

For a different, but equally striking frame design, go floral. This is easy to do using flower and leaf punches. Arrange the floral stickers in garlands around the frame.

Or, you can change shape cutter templates to alter either the frame shape or the shape of the window aperture. How about the sophisticated elegance of an oval frame? A heart-shaped window is the ideal choice for a Valentine's gift.

Or make a smaller frame for wallet-sized pictures to add a touch of elegance to all your photos.

Enlarge the pattern 118%.

# button box

**C**rafty person that I am, one of my favorite childhood playthings was the family button box. To me, it was a treasure chest! The magical contents of that button box—and my lifelong love of sewing—have inspired this cheerful paper collage box, suitable for storing sewing knickknacks in.

The button box would make a thoughtful gift for a sewing enthusiast of any age and will house a treasure trove of sewing notions. Maybe the gift will—in a small way—bring happy memories to a budding crafter.

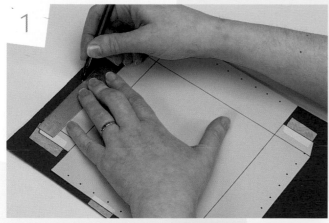

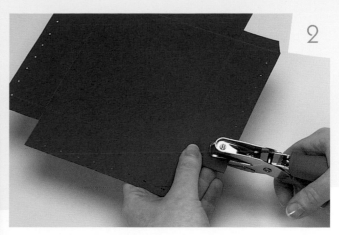

### TIP

*For the smaller paper buttons, you may find it easier to punch the holes in the cardstock first, then punch the shape out around the holes. To do this, hold the paper punch upside down and look through the cutout to position the shape over the holes.*

### 1. TRACE THE BOX LID

Enlarge the box lid template on page 111. Transfer it onto a piece of light-colored cardstock and cut it out with a craft knife and ruler. Tape the template onto the back (the smooth side) of the blue basketweave corrugated cardboard. Use a stylus to impress the pattern outlines into the cardboard (see page 16). Remember to mark the fold lines, as well as the stitching holes along the box lid edges.

### 2. CUT OUT THE BOX LID

Use a craft knife and ruler to cut out the box lid. Be sure to cut the angle corners on the flaps. Cutting corrugated cardboard requires special care. Use a fresh blade in your knife and don't apply much pressure—or the paper could catch and tear. Next, use the $1/16"$ (2mm) punch to make the stitching holes.

### 3. PUNCH OUT THE LARGE BUTTONS

Using the 1" (25mm) circle punch, punch out four circles each from red, green and yellow cardstock. Make a graph paper template, marking dots for the four center holes in each button. With the stylus, use the template to mark indentations on each paper button to indicate hole placement. Keep placement uniform for all buttons.

### 4. PUNCH OUT THE HOLES IN EACH BUTTON

With the $1/16"$ (2mm) circle punch, punch out the four holes on all of the large buttons. Use the star, heart and small circle punches to cut out a variety of smaller paper buttons. Make four or five in each color and from mirrored cardstock. Punch two holes in the smaller-size buttons.

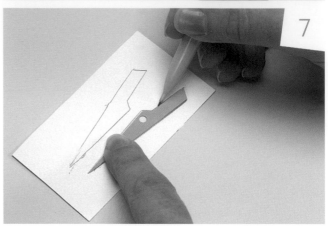
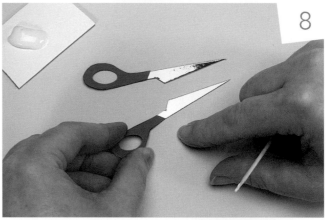

### 5. MAKE THE SPOOLS OF THREAD

Trace the cardstock template for the spool shape. Next, trace and cut out five spools from orange cardstock using a craft knife and ruler or scissors. Cut rectangular spool sized pieces of corrugated cardboard to fit the spools you just cut, making sure the ridges run horizontally across the width. This will be the thread. Cut thread rectangles in white, yellow and green—enough for all the spools. Glue the corrugated thread onto the spool.

### 6. TRACE THE SCISSORS' HANDLES

Cut out a cardstock template for the scissors' handles. Punch out two 1/2" (13mm) ovals from a piece of orange cardstock. Place the handle template over one punched oval and trace around it. Flip the template over to trace the other handle so that you have a right-facing and a left-facing handle.

### 7. TRACE THE SCISSORS' BLADES

Cut out a cardstock template for the scissors' blades. On the reverse side of the mirrored cardstock, trace the blade template. Flip the template over and trace a second blade.

### 8. ASSEMBLE THE SCISSORS' BLADES

Cut out all the scissors pieces with a craft knife and ruler for the straight lines and small scissors for the curves. Glue a handle onto each blade, as shown. Make sure the right and left sides are glued correctly. You may need to trim the base of the orange handle to fit the blade.

### 9. ASSEMBLE THE SCISSORS

Cross the left blade over the right blade and apply glue at the intersection. Next, punch out a 1/8" (3mm) circle from mirrored cardstock and glue it onto the cross point.

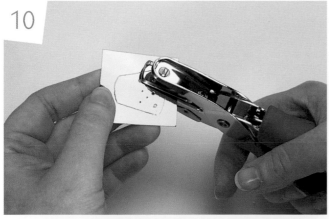

10

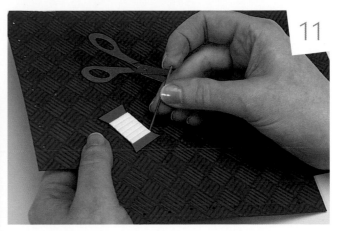

11

12

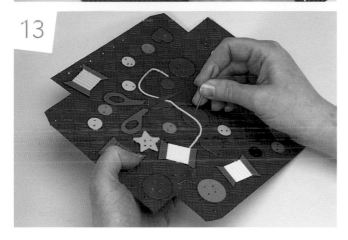

13

### 10. MAKE THE THIMBLE

Impress the thimble outline onto the back of the mirrored cardstock, marking dots for the thimble dimples. Use the $\frac{1}{16}$" (2mm) punch to punch out the thimble holes. Then cut out the thimble with scissors.

### 11. GLUE THE SPOOL AND SCISSORS

Using crafter's glue, glue the white spool of thread and the scissors onto the top of the box lid. Do not glue the uppermost blade of the scissors. With a tapestry needle, pierce a hole at the base of the spool.

### 12. ATTACH THE THREAD

Cut a piece of white velvety cord and knot the end. Push the cord up through the hole, pull it tight, then place the cord under the uppermost scissor blade so it resembles thread. Arrange the thread so it falls in a gentle curve. Glue the end of the thread onto the box, then glue down the tip of the uppermost scissor blade.

### 13. GLUE ON THE EMBELLISHMENTS

Glue the other embellishments onto the box lid. They should form a balanced arrangement of shape, size and color. For instance, on each box lid side, you should have one spool of thread and at least one large button. After all the buttons have been glued onto the box lid, take a tapestry needle and pierce the holes in the buttons through the box lid.

**TIP**

If desired, knitting yarn can be substituted for the velvety cord.

### 14. STITCH THE BUTTONS
----------------------------

Use the tapestry needle to sew velvety cord through the holes in the buttons. The cord color should contrast with the button. Sew a cross-stitch through the large red buttons. Knot thread ends on the underside of the box lid.

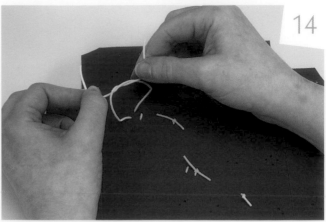

### 15. ASSEMBLE THE BOX LID
----------------------------

Crease the box lid on all the fold lines. One at a time, apply glue to the textured surface of the angled side flaps and glue them under each box side. Use a bit of masking tape to secure the flap until the glue dries. Make sure the cord knots clear the flaps.

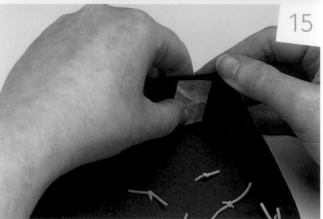

### 16. LACE THE LID BORDER
----------------------------

Thread a tapestry needle with 14" (36cm) of yellow cord. Lace the thread through the holes using an overcast stitch (that is, sewing around and around the box edge). When you run out of cord, tie on a new piece on the front of the box, then continue lacing. When you have stitched around the box, tie the cord ends together. Trim the cord ends by each knot.

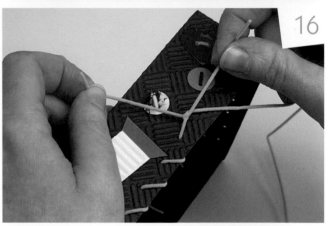

### 17. ASSEMBLE THE BOX BASE
----------------------------

Enlarge the box base pattern (on page 111) and make a cardstock pattern. Trace the box base onto a piece of red cardstock; cut it out using a craft knife held against a straightedge. Score the fold lines. Next, crease the box base along the folds. Apply glue to the flaps, and glue them behind the box base sides. Use masking tape to hold the box base in place as the glue dries. When the glue is dry, slide the box lid over the base to complete the button box.

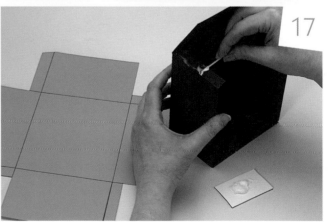

## Real Buttons

*For a realistic touch, you can sew genuine buttons onto the box lid instead of the paper ones. Choose lightweight plastic buttons, or the lid will become too weighty.*

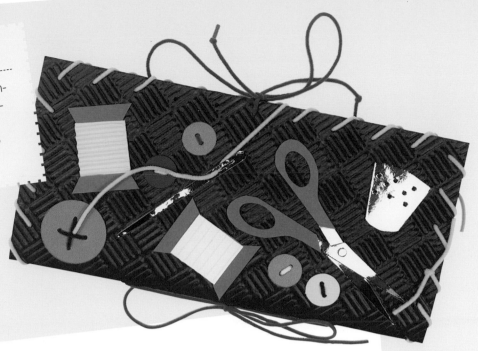

### 1. CUT OUT AND DECORATE THE NEEDLE BOOK

Enlarge the needle book pattern on page 111.
Trace it onto the smooth side of a piece of dark
red basketweave corrugated cardboard, as for
step 1 of the Button Box. Decorate the front cover
of the needle book with embellishments (thread
spools, buttons, scissors, thimble) as for the
Button Box. Next, trace the needle onto the back
of mirrored cardstock. Cut it out using a craft
knife. Then use the craft knife to cut out the eye
of the needle. Thread yellow cord through the eye
of the needle, then lace the edge of the needle
book, as for step 16 of the Button Box—only
leave the last few lacing holes unstitched on the
front cover (as if it is a work in progress). Glue
the free end of the cord inside the needle book.

## TIP

*Do not use paper edgers to cut out the felt.
They are not strong enough for the job. Use
pinking shears that are made for fabric use.*

## 2. CUT OUT THE FELT LINER

The needle book is lined with a piece of felt. This will hold the needles. Enlarge the liner template and tape it onto a piece of blue felt. Use pinking shears to cut out the felt rectangle.

## 3. ATTACH THE FELT LINER

With a tapestry needle, pierce three holes, as marked on the center fold of the needle book. Cut 18" (46cm) of blue cord. Thread a tapestry needle with the cord. Lay the felt on the back of the needle book. Sew the cord through the two end holes, so it catches in the felt and makes one long stitch across the fold on the right (basketweave) side of the needle book. On the felt side, adjust the cord ends so they are equal in length. Next, sew the cord ends through the center hole, bringing one end out to either side of the long stitch. Make a knot in the end of each cord, then tie the cord ends into a bow.

## 4. ATTACH THE TIES

Cut two 8" (20cm) pieces of blue velvet cord. Knot the end of each piece of cord. Thread a piece of cord through the center lacing hole on the front cover of the needle book. Thread the other cord through the center lacing hole on the needle book back. Make a decorative knot at the end of each cord. To fasten the needle book, tie the cords in a bow.

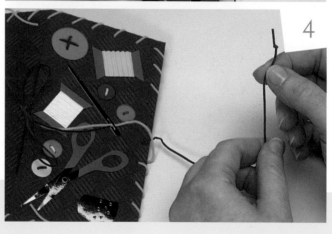

These patterns appear at full size.

LINER

Enlarge the patterns 250%

LID

NEEDLEBOOK WITH LINER

# folded star gift box & tag

The kaleidoscopic starburst design gracing the box lid is inspired by Folded Star patchwork, a needlework technique in which multilayered starbursts are built up using folded triangles of fabric.

There is a secret to constructing the seemingly intricate starburst configuration. By gluing a paper grid onto the box lid, positioning the triangles is a piece of cake and the starburst can be assembled in minutes!

This gift box is a shining example of how printed scrapbooking papers can be used to create realistic patchwork-style projects. The papercrafted Folded Star patchwork is a dead ringer for its fabric-crafted "cousin."

### 1. BASECOAT THE BOX

Use light blue acrylic paint to basecoat the box. Add a little bit of water for a creamy consistency. Paint the entire box: inside and outside, base and lid. It may take two to three coats to cover the dark color of the papier mâché box. Make sure nothing shows through.

### 2. TRACE THE PATTERN PIECE

Cut a rectangular pattern template measuring 1½" × ¾" (40mm × 20mm) out of cardstock. Use a pencil to trace around the template on the back of the printed scrapbooking paper. Mark twenty-one rectangles on the green checked paper, sixteen on the blue-background floral, and twenty-four on the white-background floral.

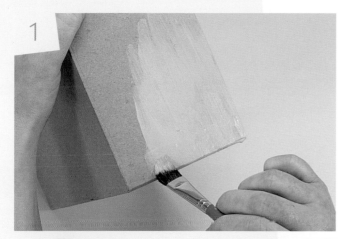

### 3. CUT OUT THE RECTANGLES

Cut out the rectangles using a craft knife held against a metal ruler.

### 4. FOLD THE TRIANGLES

Fold the rectangle in half crosswise; then fold
the top corners to meet at the bottom of the
center crease, forming the triangle. Crease the
folds sharply. Fold so the back of the paper is
on the inside.

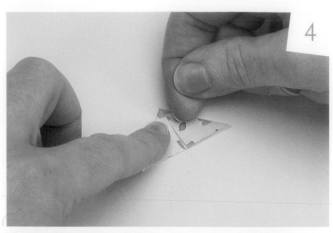

## TIP

*Store like-colored triangles together in
small plastic bags—makes for speedy selection when gluing.*

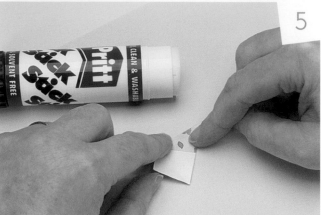

### 5. GLUE THE TRIANGLES

Apply a dry glue stick to the bottom edge of
each triangle to seal it. You will have to open
out each triangle and then refold it to do this.
Glue all the triangles in this way.

### 6. CUT OUT THE BASE FOR THE BOX LID

Mark a 5" (13cm) square on the pearlescent
blue cardstock. Use a right triangle to make
sure the corners are square. Cut out the square
using a craft knife and ruler.

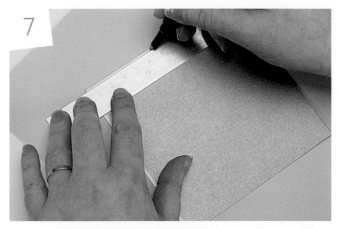

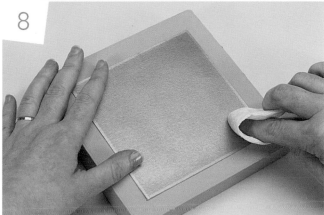

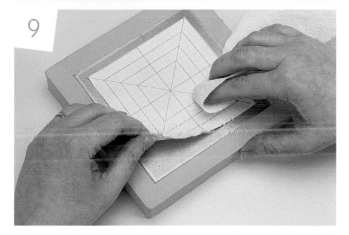

### 7. OUTLINE THE EDGES IN GOLD

Use the metallic gold fine point marker to outline the edges of the blue square. Draw against a straightedge to ensure straight lines. Wipe the straightedge clean after you mark each side.

### 8. GLUE THE BASE ONTO THE BOX LID

Measure a ⅝" (15mm) border around the box lid. With a dry glue stick, glue the base onto the box lid within the border. Smooth the base in place to prevent bubbles in the paper.

### 9. GLUE ON THE PATTERN GRID

Trace the pattern grid template (given on page 123) onto a piece of plain white paper, marking the concentric squares and the diagonals. Adjust the size of the pattern, if necessary, using a photocopier. Mark a ⅜" (10mm) border around the edge of the base. Cut out the pattern grid square, and glue it onto the base with a dry glue stick. Smooth the grid in place with a paper towel.

## Circular Starbursts

*To create round—rather than square—starburst designs, fold your triangles from semicircles of paper. Crease each semicircle in half, then fold the sides to the center, creating a "pizza slice" wedge. Glue the wedges onto a pattern grid made of concentric circles.*

### 10. APPLY GLUE TO THE TRIANGLES

Use the following gluing technique for all the paper triangles: On the back of the triangles use a toothpick to place a dab of glue near the tip of the triangle and also apply a line of glue sparingly along the base.

### 11. APPLY THE CENTER TRIANGLES

For the first round of the design, glue on four green triangles, one on each side of the square in the center of the grid. The triangle tips face the grid center, and each base is placed on the first grid line.

### 12. START THE SECOND ROUND

To begin the second round, glue on four blue triangles. The point of each triangle belongs on the center line of each side, and the base belongs on the second grid line.

## Tea Bag Paper Extravaganza

For a fantastic, superdeluxe kaleidoscope effect, make your starburst triangles out of tea bag folding papers with "engineered" border designs. Position the printed paper differently for the triangles of each round.

10

11

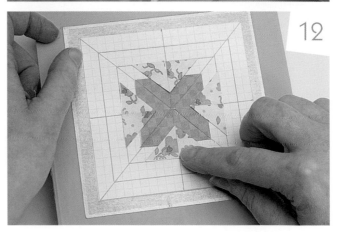

12

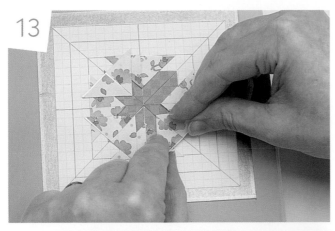

### 13. COMPLETE THE SECOND ROUND

To finish the round, you need four more blue triangles. Glue a blue triangle diagonally across each corner. The tips of corner triangles should be placed at the same level as those glued on in the previous step.

### 14. GLUE THE THIRD ROUND

For the third round, you need twelve green triangles, three evenly spaced on each side. Start with the left-hand triangle on each side. Glue it so that its left-hand edge is on the corner diagonal and its base is on the third grid line. Overlap the next triangle, gluing it so that the left-hand tip lies at the midpoint of the previous triangle, and its center lies at the center of the grid side. Lap the third triangle over the second triangle to complete the side. The right-hand side of the triangle should align with the corner diagonal. Work your way around the grid, gluing the triangles in a counterclockwise direction until the third round is complete.

### 15. GLUE ON THE FOURTH ROUND

You need sixteen white triangles for the fourth—and final—round of the starburst. Glue the triangles as you did for the previous round, overlapping each successive triangle, but use four on each side. Along the baseline, position the left-hand tip of each triangle at the midpoint of the previous triangle. Work in a counterclockwise direction to complete the round.

### 16. OUTLINE THE EDGE

Use the gold marker to decoratively outline the edges of the starburst. This will conceal any ragged edges. Use a straightedge to keep the lines crisp and even. Wipe the straightedge clean after each side.

### 17. PIERCE A HOLE

For the beads, use a tapestry needle to pierce a hole through the center point of the starburst, penetrating the box beneath. The papier-mâché is pretty soft, and you will be able to work the needle through. If one is handy, a bradawl would be a more effective tool for the job. Place a piece of kneaded eraser underneath to catch the point.

### 18. THREAD THE BEADS

Thread the 1/8" (3mm) bead on the gold wire by hand and place it at the center of the wire. Next, thread both wire ends through a sewing needle and draw it through the 1/4" (6mm) gold bead.

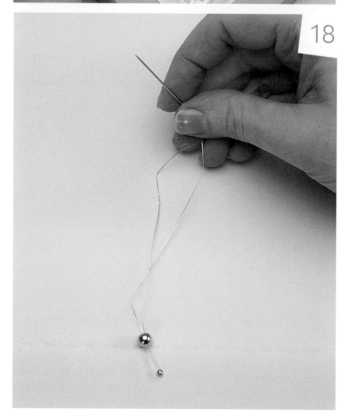

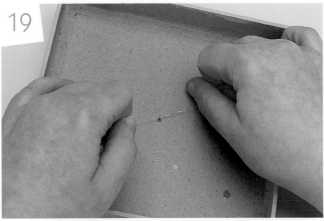

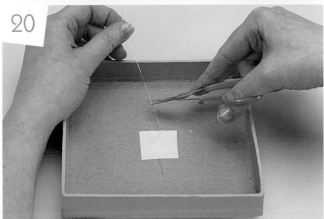

### 19. ATTACH THE BEAD
---

Draw the bead wire through the hole in the box, pull it tight, then knot it in place several times.

### 20. SECURE THE BEADS
---

Spread the bead wire open, ends apart, then apply crafter's glue to the underside of the bead hole. Affix a self-adhesive label over the hole, then trim off the gold wire thread, letting it extend a little beyond the label.

### 21. OUTLINE THE TOP EDGES OF THE LID
---

With the gold marker, rule decorative lines on the top edges of the box lid. Do this on all four sides. Wipe the straightedge clean after each side.

### 22. DECORATE THE LID SIDES
---

Decorate the box lid sides by gluing on a border of overlapping triangles. You need six triangles for each side, two in each color. Each left-hand triangle tip should touch the center line of the previous triangle. Make sure the triangles fill the entire lid side; you might have to fudge the spacing a little to ensure this. When the border is complete, use a ruler to make a gold marker line along the bottom edge.

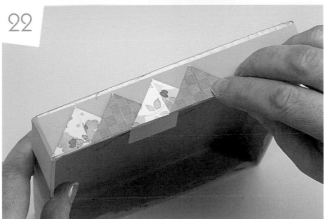

### 23. CREATE THE BOX BANDS
----------------------

Cut out four bands from pearlescent blue card-stock, each measuring ¾" (20mm) wide by 5¾" (15cm) long—the length of the box side. Line the top and bottom on each band with gold marker.

### 24. ATTACH THE BANDS
----------------------

Measure up ¾" (19mm) from the bottom of the box. Use crafter's glue to attach a band onto each side of the box. Make sure the bands fit the box sides; trim them if necessary. Use a paper towel to smooth the band down.

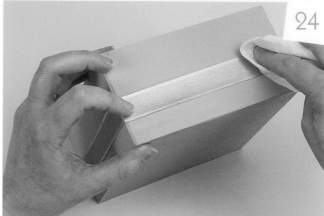

# Patchwork Gift Tag

The following steps are for making a patchwork gift tag for your box, but this tag certainly isn't just for this box. It will make an excellent addition to any gift packaging you do, from presents to gift bags!

### 1. MAKE THE GIFT TAG
----------------------

Measure and cut out a 3⅛" (8cm) square from the green pearlescent cardstock. Outline the tag edges with gold marker.

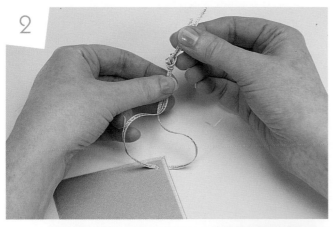

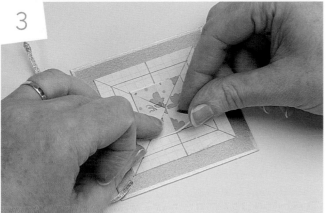

## 2. ATTACH THE RIBBON
----------------------

Punch a ⅛" (3mm) hole in the corner of the tag. Cut a 12" (30cm) piece of ⅛" (3mm) wide gold taffeta ribbon; thread it through the hole and knot the ends together. Trim off the ribbon ends.

### TIP

Create a grid for the gift tag pattern by reducing the grid for the Folded Star Gift Box by 25% and trim the grid so that you are using only three rounds.

## 3. GLUE ON THE PLACEMENT GRID
----------------------------------

Glue the grid onto the tag, placing it ⅜" (10mm) from the tag edges. The triangles for the tag are folded from rectangles 1¼" (30mm) long by ⅝" (15mm) wide. You need four blue triangles, eight blue-check triangles and nine white triangles. Glue on the first round of blue triangles, as for step 11.

## 4. FINISH THE STARBURST
---------------------------

Continue gluing triangles to complete the pattern. Attach round 2 (blue checks), as for steps 12–13. Attach round 3 (the final round), as for step 14. Use white triangles. The gift tag starburst has only three rounds.

## 5. DECORATE THE TAG
-----------------------

Use the gold marker to outline the edges of the starburst. Punch a ⅛" (3mm) dot from matte gold paper and glue it onto the starburst center.

## ❀ VARIATION IDEA: NESTED BOXES

A set of boxes in graduated sizes—like Russian dolls—makes a charming gift. Papier-mâché boxes come in standard sizes of 4" (10cm), 6" (15cm) and 8" (20cm). The pattern should be reduced 25% for the smaller box. The small and large starbursts are constructed in exactly the same way as for the illustrated project (the medium-size box); only, the triangles should be enlarged 50% for the large box. The starburst for the small box lid is the same as for the gift tag; it has just three rounds of triangles.

Small box: 4" (10cm)
Lid base: 3⅛" (8cm) square
Side band: ½" (13mm) wide by 3¾" (10cm) long, ½" (13mm) above box base

Large box: 8" (20cm)
Lid base: 7" (18cm)
Side band: ⅞" (22mm) wide by 7¾" (20cm) long, 1" (25mm) above box base

The details for the medium box are given in the project instructions.

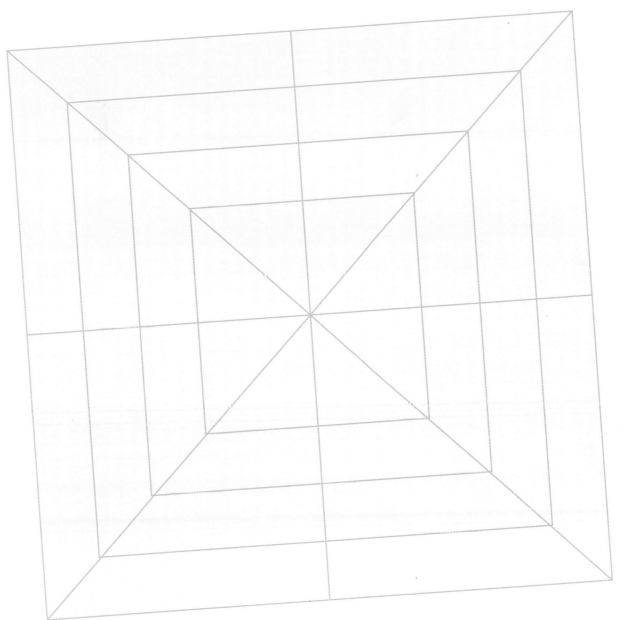

The following pattern is for the large
box. Reduce by 50% for the medium box.

The following pattern
is for the medium
size box.

# Resources

## Artbase

88 North Street
Hornchurch
Essex RM11 1SR
UK
Tel: 01708 457 948
Fax: 01708 457 949
E-mail: artbasehx@aol.com
www.artbasehornchurch.com

* Mail-order suppliers of scrapbooking materials. They stock
DMC Fantasy Velvet craft cord.

## Creative Xpress!!

295 West Center Street
Provo, UT 84601
Tel: (800)563-8679
Fax: (801)373-1446
www.creativexpress.com

* Mail-order suppliers of craft
materials, including scrapbooking supplies and the Coluzzle
cutting system.

## Daler-Rowney USA

2 Corporate Drive
Cranbury, NJ 08512-9584
Tel: (609) 655-5252
Fax: (609) 655-5852
www.daler-rowney.com

* Manufacturers of artists'
materials, including Canford
colored paper and card stock.

## EK Success

125 Entin Road
Clifton, NJ 07014
E-mail:
success@eksuccess.com
www.eksuccess.com

* Manufacturers of scrapbooking supplies, including Paper
Shapers punches and Zig
Memory System archival quality markers. Product info only.

## Fiskars Brands, Inc.

7811 West Stewart Avenue
Wausau, WI 54401
Tel: (800)950-0203
Fax: (715) 848-3657
www.fiskars.com

* Manufacturers of Fiskars
paper-cutting products, including paper edgers, hand punches
and the ShapeCutter. Web site
includes how-to tips and project ideas.

## Olfa

1536 Beech Street
Terra Haute, IN 47804
Tel: (800) 962-OLFA
Fax: (866) 800-6532
www.olfa.com
* Manufacturers of cutting
tools; craft knives, compass-
style circle cutter.

## Origami 4 You

Tel: +44 (0) 7971 083069
E-mail:
info@origami4you.com
www.origami4you.co.uk

* Mail-order origami resource.

## Paper Adventures

P.O. Box 04393
Milwaukee, WI 53204-0393
Tel: (800) 727-0699
Fax: (800) 727-0268
www.paperadventures.com

* Manufacturers of acid-free
scrapbooking papers. No shopping from the Web site, but an
inspirational browse!

## Pilot Pen Corporation

Customer Service
Department
60 Commerce Drive
Trumbull, CT 06611
Tel: (203) 377-8800
Fax: (203) 377-4024
E-mail: service@pilotpen.com
www.pilotpen.com

*Manufacturers of gel ink
pens, Super Color Gold markers
and more.*

## Phrazzle Card Limited

Phrazzle House
29 Hest View Road
Ulverston
Cumbria LA12 9PH
UK
Tel: +44 (0) 1229 588880
www.phrazzlecard.co.uk

*Mail-order supplier of
pearlescent paper and corrugated cardboard.*

## Sakura of America, Inc.

30780 San Clemente Street
Hayward, CA 94544
Tel: (510) 475-8880
Fax: (510) 475-0973
Email: express@sakurao-
famerica.com
www.gellyroll.com

*Manufacturers of archival-
quality pens, including Pigma
Micron pens.*

## USArtQuest, Inc.

7800 Ann Arbor Road
Grass Lake, MI 49240
Tel: (517) 522-6225
Fax: (517) 522-6228
E-mail:
askanything@usartquest.com
www.usartquest.com

*Manufacturer and mail-order
supplier of acid-free, archival-
quality and nontoxic Perfect
Paper Adhesive.*

## Uchida of America, Corp.

3535 Del Amo Boulevard
Torrance, CA 90503
Tel: (800) 541-5877
Fax: (800) 229-7017
E-mail: marvy@uchida.com
www.uchida.com

*Manufacturers of craft sup-
plies, including craft punches.
Can buy direct from the Web
site.*

## Xyron, Inc.

15820 North 84th Street
Scottsdale, AZ 85260
Tel: (800) 793-3523
Fax: (480) 443-0118
E-mail: info@xyron.com
www.xyron.com

*Manufacturers of laminating
machines. Web site includes
how-tos and project ideas.*

# Index

# Get creative with North Light Books!

## The Essential Guide to Handmade Books

Gabrielle Fox teaches you how to create your own handmade books—one-of-a-kind art pieces that go beyond the standard definition of what a "book" can be. You'll find 11 projects inside. Each one builds upon the next, just as your skills increase. This beginner-friendly progression ensures that you're well prepared to experiment, play and design your own unique handmade books.

*ISBN 1-58180-019-3, paperback, 128 pages, #31652-K*

## The Big Book of Greeting Cards

This book presents a variety of fun, festive and stylish ideas for making cards perfect for any occasion. Discover more than 40 step-by-step projects using a wide range of techniques including rubber stamping, stenciling, quilling and embroidery.

*ISBN 1-58180-323-0, paperback, 144 pages, #32287-K*

## How to Be Creative if You Never Thought You Could

Let Tera Leigh act as your personal craft guide and motivator. She'll help you discover just how creative you really are. You'll explore eight exciting crafts through 16 fun, fabulous projects, including rubber stamping, bookmaking, papermaking, collage, decorative painting and more. Tera prefaces each new activity with insightful essays and encouraging advice.

*ISBN 1-58180-293-5, paperback, 128 pages, #32170-K*

## Stenciling & Embossing Greeting Cards

Judy Barker introduces you to the basics of stenciling and embossing attractive greeting cards. You'll also learn how to embellish them with foil, polymer clay, shrink plastic and more. It's everything you need to make one-of-a-kind cards for family and friends alike.

*0-89134-997-9, paperback, 128 pages, #31613-K*